ANTI-INFLAMMATORY DIET COOKBOOK

for Beginners

2000+ Days of Amazing Mouthwatering Recipes

Strengthen Your Immune System

Decrease In lammation

Detox Your Body

and Balance Hormones in 9 Days

ISABELLA WILLIAMS

CONTENTS

INTRODUCTION

Inflammation is seen as a threat to health by many people. However, inflammation is a normal part of your body's defense system. Inflammation is typically the result of a cascade of chemical reactions triggered by hormones in the body's attempt to rid itself of infections or restore chemical equilibrium. Pain and inflammation are indicators that there is a problem with our bodies. This may result from a nutritional deficiency, an excess accumulation of nutrients, or an attack by pathogens. Diabetes, cancer, heart disease, COPD, and Alzheimer's disease are just some diseases linked to inflammation in the body.

On the other hand, many things have been shown to help reduce and even cure inflammation. Reducing stress, maintaining a regular exercise routine, and making healthy food choices are all good places to start. The food we eat greatly affects the way our bodies function. That's because what we put into our bodies profoundly affects how they function, and avoiding inflammatory foods can help alleviate a wide range of health problems.

Adhering to certain dietary guidelines can alleviate inflammation and other disease symptoms. For example, anti-inflammatory diets have been shown to effectively lower inflammation levels. These diets focus on supplying the body with nutrients while providing soothing chemicals to reduce inflammation.

This book provides a systematic method for improving one's diet and way of life through an anti-inflammatory diet and everything you need to get started. Of course, the more information you have, the closer you will get to your goal. All the best!

Chapter 1

What is Anti-Inflammatory Diet?

There is a lot of conflicting information about what inflammation is. How anti-inflammatory diet works? Which foods to eat and avoid? In this detailed guide, we draw from the most recent and relevant research to give you the information you need to move forward confidently with your anti-inflammatory diet journey. Maintaining healthy, well-balanced eating habits in adults, adolescents, and children can be simplified by adopting an anti-inflammatory diet.

1.1 What Is Inflammation?

What comes to mind when you think of inflammation? Most people associate inflammation with redness, swelling, heat, and pain, but inflammation can originate from within the body and cause nearly all diseases seen today. Before we get into how you can make dietary changes to help combat systemic inflammation, it's important to understand what happens inside your body when inflammation occurs. If you understand what inflammation is and what causes it, you will be well on your way to protecting your body from inflammatory diseases.

The first thing to realize is that not all inflammation is harmful. Inflammation is a normal part of the healing process and can help the body fight infection and disease. Acute inflammation, such as when you get a wound, aids in the healing process. Irritation is the first stage of inflammation, followed by inflammation and pus discharge from a wound. Then, the granulation stage follows, during which round masses of tissue form during the healing process. All you need to remember from this process is that wounds will never heal without inflammation.

There are two types of inflammation;

Acute inflammation and chronic inflammation

Acute inflammation is defined by its rapid onset and severity. The symptoms and signs last only a few days, but sometimes they can last for weeks.

The following are some conditions, diseases, and situations that can cause acute inflammation:
- Infected ingrown toenail
- A scratch/cut on the skin
- Acute bronchitis
- Acute appendicitis
- Sore throat from a cold or flu
- Acute dermatitis
- Exercise (especially intense training)
- Acute infective meningitis
- A blow
- Acute tonsillitis
- Acute sinusitis

Chronic inflammation refers to long-term inflammation. Chronic inflammation is much more than just a few days. It can, in fact, last for months or even years. Chronic inflammation can occur due to an autoimmune reaction, a chronic irritant, or continuing to consume the irritant that caused the inflammation in the first place. It can be caused by:

- Failure to remove the source of the acute inflammation
- An autoimmune response to a self-antigen occurs when the immune system combats healthy tissue by mistaking them for dangerous pathogens.
- A low-intensity chronic irritant that persists.

Chronic inflammatory diseases and conditions include the following:

- Asthma
- Chronic sinusitis
- Tuberculosis
- Chronic peptic ulcer
- Rheumatoid arthritis
- Ulcerative colitis and Crohn's disease
- Chronic sinusitis
- Chronic periodontitis
- Chronic active hepatitis (there are many more)

Without inflammation, our wounds, infections, and tissue damage would never heal - tissue would become increasingly harmed, and the body, or any organism, would gradually perish.

Chronic inflammation, on the other hand, can lead to various conditions and diseases, including some atherosclerosis, cancers, periodontitis, rheumatoid arthritis, and hay fever. Therefore, inflammation must be well controlled.

The bottom line is that chronic inflammation can harm one's health. Therefore, making dietary and lifestyle changes is essential to controlling inflammation. With inflammation being the root cause of nearly all diseases, we must all do our part to protect our health through the food we eat.

Let's look at the causes and symptoms of inflammation now that you know more about it and the distinction between acute and chronic inflammation.

Inflammation Symptoms

Heat, redness, swelling, pain, and muscle function loss are the most common symptoms of inflammation. The inflamed body part and the cause of the inflammation determine these symptoms. Some common symptoms of chronic inflammation include:

- Recurrent infections
- Increased weight.
- Physical discomfort.
- Sleeplessness

- Tiredness
- Anxiety and depression are examples of mood disorders.
- Digestive issues such as diarrhea, constipation, and acid reflux disease

Various inflammatory effect issues cause the typical symptoms of inflammation. For example, rashes occur when the body's defense mechanisms attack the skin. When you have rheumatoid arthritis, it affects your joints. The most common signs and symptoms are fatigue, tingling, joint pains, stiffness, and swelling.

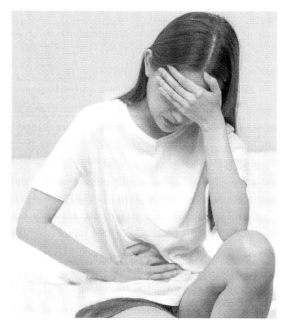

Similarly, when you have inflammatory bowel disease, it usually affects your digestive system. Bleeding ulcers, anemia, diarrhea, weight loss, bloating, and stomach pains are common symptoms. Multiple sclerosis is a condition that affects the myelin sheath, which covers the nerve cells. Its symptoms include difficulty passing stool, double vision, blurred vision, fatigue, and cognitive issues.

You may suffer from inflammation if you experience any of the following symptoms and health issues. Many people associate it with joint pains such as arthritis, characterized by swelling and aches. However, the issue is related to more than just swollen joints. Nonetheless, not all pain is bad. For example, acute inflammation is critical during a twisted and puffy ankle recovery.

Chronic inflammation symptoms and causes are simple to identify. It can be caused by insomnia, genetic predisposition, food intake, and other personal habits. Similarly, allergic inflammation can cause inflammation in your gut.

The following are some of the possibilities:
- If you are constantly tired to the point of not getting enough sleep, taking enough naps, or sleeping excessively.
- Do you get aches and pains from time to time? It could also indicate that you have arthritis.
- Do you have any abdominal pain or a stomachache? Inflammation may result from the pain. Cramping, bloating, and loose stools can all be symptoms of gut inflammation.
- Another sign of inflammation is a swollen lymph node. These nodes are located in the neck, armpits, and groin and swell if your system malfunctions. For example, when you have a sore throat, your neck nodes swell because your body's defense system has detected the problem. Because the body is fighting the infection, these lymph nodes react. As you heal, the nodes reshape.
- Do you have a stuffy nose? If so, it could be a symptom of irritating nasal tooth cavities.
- Internal inflammation can cause your epidermis to protrude.

1.2 Six Inflammation Causes

Chronic inflammation, the ultimate cause of several serious diseases, is caused by several factors. First, inflammation can occur at any time of day: what is eaten for breakfast, lunch, and dinner, what is breathed in and exhaled out, and what is accumulated in the form of emotions or injuries. And if not treated properly, inflammation can cause havoc in the body.

Toxicity

Toxicity has been linked to inflammation. But where does toxicity originate? A team of scientists recently conducted a study and discovered chemicals stored in various body cells. These chemicals included flame retardants and Bisphenol A, a hormone-like chemical in plastics. These chemicals are derived from the environment and serve no purpose in the body. As a result, the body works against them, rushing pathogen-fighting cells to combat them. However, the environment remains unchanged. For example, a person constantly breathes in and out, and the things that arrive in that breath are toxic. Furthermore, certain food products contain several indigestible toxins.

Infection that lasts a long time

As previously stated, infection can result in immediate inflammation. Infection, contrary to popular belief, is not the same as inflammation. Infection occurs when pathogens attempt to reproduce and rampage in a specific area of cells. This infection absorbs all of the oxygen and nutrients available in this area. When inflammation takes hold, however, it summons immediate pathogen-fighting mechanisms to the scene. Following that, the infection appears red and swollen. Chronic infection, on the other hand, can cause chronic inflammation. Chronic infection can go completely undetected. Hepatitis C, for example, affects the liver and can be present for years without causing symptoms. Chronic inflammation, on the other hand, is raging alongside this chronic infection. The two are fighting and draining excessive resources from the body, resulting in perpetual illness.

Allergens

An allergic reaction is an overreaction of the body's immune system. The allergen is usually harmless; however, the body's inflammation immediately kicks in and attempts to attack it, resulting in inflammatory symptoms. Allergens from food and the environment both contribute to inflammation. Many people, for example, have gluten intolerance, which is the inability to digest gluten found in bread and pastries. Gluten, on the other hand, is a protein that should be beneficial to the body. When gluten enters their bodies, they immediately develop an allergic reaction. This allergic reaction is inflammatory. A person suffering from gluten intolerance may experience aches and pains, irritable bowel syndrome, or diarrhea. However, allergic inflammation can manifest as itching and scratching from a bug bite or poison ivy exposure. The allergen is not harmful, but the body does not recognize this. As a result, the inflammatory response persists.

Poor Nutrition

To avoid inflammatory responses, proper nutritional intake must be maintained. Several of the foods discussed in this book cause inflammatory responses. Sugary foods are the most heinous offenders. Sugar can cause damage to the stomach and digestive tract lining. This causes immediate inflammatory reactions. A sugar-laden diet, on the other hand, is relentless. Furthermore, a high-sugar diet raises insulin levels in the blood. A high insulin blood level causes a variety of imbalances, and the inflammatory response works to regulate the body.

Injury

An injury can also cause chronic inflammation. The first bodily response to injury is, of course, inflammation. The body adheres to the exact mechanics of acute inflammation. The body enables us to perceive pain, swelling, and heat. When other environmental factors (such as poor diet, chronic stress, or toxicity) enter the picture, our initial injury inflammation can continue to interact in the body. As a result, chronic inflammation can occur, leading to additional problems.

Prolonged Stress

Chronic stress occurs when we are constantly in a state of fight-or-flight: when we never take the time to relax from the tasks. Of course, fight-or-flight responses are advantageous. They are caused by the hormone cortisol pulsing via the bloodstream, allowing for increased motivation and alertness. However, when cortisol levels in the bloodstream remain high, the body begins to fight against itself. Researchers have shown chronic stress to alter the genes of immune cells. The change forces them to be in constant combat mode. Immune cells, which are normally activated in the inflammatory response, are thus constantly on duty, leading to chronic inflammation.

1.3 What is Anti-Inflammatory Diet?

Inflammation is a normal and natural part of the body's healing process. Inflammation occurs when the body needs to defend itself against something foreign. The issue is that it has the potential to become a chronic issue. When a person has chronic inflammation, it can last for weeks, months, or years. This can then lead to other serious health issues. The good news is that there are numerous things that a person can do to help reduce inflammation. A person can feel perfectly normal while having significant inflammation.

There is no fancy or catchy name for the anti-inflammatory diet. Nothing will tell you you will lose a dress size in a week. Essentially, it is a lifestyle and eating plan rather than a diet. Any anti-inflammatory diet on the market is derived from the same neighborhood. They will benefit the user's overall health. The diet can help lower blood pressure and triglycerides, control existing cardiac issues, lower the risk of heart disease, and soothe arthritic joints. Although you may lose weight while on the anti-inflammatory diet, it is not solely for weight loss; it is not a three-week journey to remove existing inflammation from the body. It is not a quick fix for health. Instead, it offers a distinct, new approach to your life: a way of life that includes all of the nutrients and minerals, calories, and proteins required to live well and happily. The anti-inflammatory diet components will help improve your overall health by providing the nutrients and inflammation-fighting compounds your body requires to heal itself and maintain proper balance. You will begin to notice changes in your appearance and mood. You will experience a surge of energy. Your skin will have a noticeable healthy glow.

Your body will function properly, producing new healthy cells and calming the chaos of inflammation in your system. To benefit from the anti-inflammatory diet, you must first understand yourself.

The average American consumes far too many foods high in omega-6 fatty acids. These are commonly found in fast food restaurants and processed foods. They don't eat enough omega-3 fatty acids, which are found in supplements and cold water fish. If the food balance is off, inflammation will begin to develop.

This diet is the polar opposite of the typical American diet. The majority of the foods that should be consumed are carbs, healthy monounsaturated fats, and low-fat proteins.

Depending on your activity level, weight, and gender, you consume 2000 to 3000 calories per day. The diet is inspired by the Mediterranean diet. More guidelines will be found as you progress through the various dietary components. You want to consume carbohydrates that will help to lower and stabilize your blood sugar.

The good news is that this diet is entirely free of charge. The only thing you need to buy is the food you eat. You are not required to pay a monthly website or subscription fee. The money you spend on the diet goes towards the food you eat and any books you may purchase to learn more.

Chronic inflammation has been linked to various serious diseases over the years. Alzheimer's disease, many cancers, and heart disease are among them. Chronic inflammation can be caused by factors such as a lack of exercise, stress, toxin exposure, and genetic predisposition, but it has also been discovered that food consumption plays a significant role. Understanding how foods affect the inflammatory process is essential for learning how to control and reduce disease risks.

This diet was not created to help people lose weight, though you will most likely lose weight, and it is not a short-term eating plan. Instead, it teaches you how to buy and prepare foods that help reduce inflammation. The food options are based on scientific evidence of what they can do to help your body maintain optimal health.

The anti-inflammatory diet can also provide protective phytonutrients, essential dietary fiber and fatty acids, minerals, vitamins, and consistent energy.

This diet aims to add variety by consuming as many different fresh foods as possible, limiting fast and processed foods, and eating more vegetables and fruits.

Why should you follow an anti-inflammatory diet?

While chronic inflammation can be caused by various factors such as stress, tobacco smoke, toxins, and triggers, dietary choices also play a significant role in inflammation. The increased consumption of processed foods has resulted in a significant increase in inflammatory diseases and disorders.

An anti-inflammatory diet (AID) is not a diet in the traditional sense, where you go on it to lose weight. This diet is more about having the knowledge and motivation to prepare foods in a scientific manner that allows your body to function optimally. This has the added benefit of assisting you in losing excess weight and getting into proper shape.

An AID's primary goal is to reduce inflammation, but it also provides your body with a steady supply of energy, vitamins, and minerals, as well as all the other essentials, such as fiber, fatty acids, and other nutrients, to keep your body functioning at its best. The diet allows for a wide variety of as fresh as possible foods. The diet also reduces the amount of junk and processed food consumed and increases fruit and vegetable consumption to supplement the body's growth and healing.

What are the benefits of following an anti-inflammatory diet?

This diet has numerous advantages because it reduces inflammation. Many health problems are caused by inflammation, and an anti-inflammatory diet works at the root to prevent these problems. As the name implies, it can help with joint pain, diabetes, heart disease, arthritis, and various other health issues. Inflammation symptoms include swelling, reddening, pain in finger joints, immobility in joints, and rigidity. An anti-inflammatory diet can also aid in their prevention.

Is there anything negative about the anti-inflammatory diet?

This diet has no significant side effects. This diet is primarily a change in our eating habits. However, studies have shown that it may result in glowing and radiant skin, weight loss, and increased energy. The side effects are hardly harmful.

1.4 How to Adhere to an Anti-Inflammatory Diet

To be effective, an anti-inflammatory diet must follow a few guidelines. They are, however, not overly complicated once you get used to them! This section will teach you the fundamentals of anti-inflammatory dieting, as well as what to eat and what to avoid.

Here are some pointers to keep in mind as you plan your diet:

- Consume a wide variety of fresh foods. The more variety you have, especially when it comes to fruits and vegetables, the better. If you have the opportunity to buy farm-fresh foods, do so; if not, try to eat fresh as often as possible.
- Aim for between 2000 and 3000 calories per day. If you're not very active or are small, you should be on the lower end of this range.
- Consume the recommended amount of each food group. Each meal should include fat, a carbohydrate, and a protein source. If you consume 2,000 calories per day, you should consume 200 grams of carbohydrates, 70 grams of fat, 100 grams of protein, and 40 grams of fiber.
- Drink plenty of tea and avoid coffee. Switching from coffee to tea as your caffeine source can help you fight cancer and heart disease. Green and white teas are the healthiest, but all teas are beneficial.
- Take fish oil supplements in addition to your diet. Alternatively, you can include oily fish in your diet twice a week.
- Consume plenty of water. When you're thirsty, drink water instead of soda. You'll be doing yourself a favor just by making this simple change!

Principles of an anti-inflammatory diet in general:

- Eat only organically grown foods to reduce your pesticide exposure. Reduce the number of food additives and colorings consumed while increasing the amount of beneficial vitamins, minerals, and antioxidants consumed, which the body uses to fight cancer and chronic disease.
- There is no set limit to how much food you can eat, and there is no requirement to track calories.
- Pay attention to your body's satiety cues.
- Eat when you're hungry and stop when you're full.
- Aim for caloric compositions of 40 percent carbohydrates, 30 percent protein, and 30 percent healthy fats when planning meals.
- Make a meal plan ahead of time.

When it comes to getting the most out of your diet, your lifestyle habits are also important.

Anti-Inflammatory Diet Dos and Don'ts

Do's of the Anti-Inflammatory Diet:

- Consume enough omega-3 fatty acids.

- From time to time, indulge in dark chocolate and red wine. Just make sure it's at least 70% dark cocoa and unsweetened.
- Consume healthy fats like olive oil, coconut oil, nuts, seeds, and avocados.
- Make sure you get plenty of rest.
- Get plenty of exercise throughout the day.
- Manage your stress levels.

Anti-inflammatory Diet Don'ts:

- Avoid eating processed junk foods.
- Avoid consuming contaminated oils.
- Don't smoke or expose yourself to toxins.
- Avoid using toxic household cleaners.
- Avoid processed and artificial sweeteners.
- Limit your intake of caffeine and alcohol.

1.5 Foods to Avoid

In the previous sections, we discussed how our eating habits and the foods we eat can cause inflammation. One way to get started on the anti-inflammatory diet is to avoid eating foods that cause inflammation.

These foods are classified into six categories:

- Foods High in Fructose and Sugar
- Vegetable Oils (Includes Seed Oils)
- Excessive alcohol consumption
- Processed Meat
- Refined Carbohydrates
- Artificial Trans Fats
- Avoid using toxic household cleaners.
- Avoid processed and artificial sweeteners.
- Limit your intake of caffeine and alcohol.

Let's go over each of these items in detail and explain why they can cause inflammation.

1. Foods High in Fructose and Sugar

Sugary foods and foods containing a lot of fructose are at the top of our list of foods to avoid. In our daily diet, there are two main culprits that contribute to inflammation.

The first is high fructose corn syrup, while the second is table sugar. These are the two most common types of sugar in our modern diet. According to one study, these added sugars cause significant harm to the body.

Another study found that eating a high sucrose diet can lead to breast cancer. Sucrose is a type of sugar. It is also suggested that eating sugary foods may delay or block omega-3 fatty acid anti-inflammatory effects.

Fructose and the other sugars found naturally in all of our foods are not inherently bad or evil. They're actually beneficial because they provide the body with the energy it requires. What's dangerous is taking in too much, which can happen quickly.

Simply drinking a large can of Coke will provide your body with all of the sugar it requires in one week in one sitting. Do you, however, stop at one can of soda? Some people consume three or more sodas per day.

Chronic diseases such as cancer, fatty liver disease, diabetes, insulin resistance, obesity, and chronic kidney disease have been linked to high fructose intake.

Foods with high levels of added sugar include the following:

- Specific types of cereals
- Delectable pastries
- Doughnuts
- Cakes
- Cookies
- Soda beverages
- Chocolates
- Candy
- Juices from fruits and vegetables (sweetened ones)
- Any sugar-sweetened beverages

2. Vegetable Oils (Includes Seed Oils)

The average consumption of vegan oils and seed oils has risen by up to 130% in the twentieth century. According to experts, it contributes to the growing number of health problems caused by inflammation. According to researchers, increased consumption of these oils causes inflammation.

These oils are high in omega-6 fatty acids. Even though they are required by the human body, they actually increase inflammation when there is more omega-6 in the body than omega-3.
It should be noted that vegetable oils are utilized in cooking and are also found in many processed foods. Reduce your intake of vegetable oils and seed oils to prevent or reduce inflammation in the body.

3. Excessive alcohol consumption

There may be some health benefits from moderate alcohol consumption. That means that a couple of drinks every now and then isn't all that bad. However, consuming more alcohol than usual can lead to serious health issues such as inflammation.

People who drink excessively may accumulate bacterial toxins in their bodies, a condition known as leaky gut syndrome. This condition can cause organ damage as well as widespread inflammation.

4. Processed Meat

Beef jerky, smoked meat, bacon, ham, and sausages are examples of processed meat. They're delicious, and some people have made them dinner table staples. However, research indicates that these foods are linked to an increased risk of a number of diseases, including colon cancer, diabetes, stomach cancer, and heart disease.

Colon cancer is the most common disease linked to processed meat consumption. Researchers believe this is because these meats contain a high concentration of advanced glycation end products or AGEs. When meat is paired with other substances and then heated to high temperatures, AGEs form.

AGEs cause inflammation in the body, according to research. It is important to note that many factors contribute to the development of colon cancer. However, research indicates that the most significant contributing factor is most likely the consumption of processed meat and the associated inflammation.

5. Refined Carbohydrates

Not all carbohydrates are created equal. Some are nice to have, while others can be a healthy part of your diet. The ones that are nice to have aren't necessarily necessary—I'm talking about refined carbohydrates.

It should be noted that not all carbohydrates are harmful. Man has been consuming carbohydrates since the dawn of time. It's true, but our forefathers ate unprocessed carbs that were high in fiber, which is beneficial to the body.

What has changed in the last century or so is the introduction of refined carbohydrates. The idea behind using refined carbohydrates is that the refining process extends the shelf life of the carbs we normally produce.

However, during the refinement process, the fiber and all other essential nutrients are removed. What remains are refined carbohydrates. Sure, they have a much longer shelf life, but studies show that they can cause a lot of inflammation.

Remember that fiber helps with blood sugar control and makes you feel full. That is why, after a high-fiber diet, you do not crave more food. Fiber also feeds the beneficial bacteria in your gut, which aids in overall health.

Why are refined carbohydrates unhealthy? According to research, the bacteria in your gut that cause inflammation feed on refined carbohydrates. When inflammation in the gut becomes chronic as a result of years of poor eating habits, it becomes a problem.

Refined carbohydrates have a higher glycemic index (GI) than unprocessed carbohydrates. Food with a high GI can cause your blood sugar to rise much faster. According to research, eating a lot of high-GI foods may cause chronic obstructive pulmonary disease.

6. Artificial Trans Fats

Artificial trans fats are the unhealthiest fats on the planet. These are products containing partially hydrogenated ingredients. That is, unsaturated fats are given a hydrogen boost. Unsaturated fats are typically liquid. They become more solid and stable when hydrogen is added to them.

These are the ingredients that have the words "partially hydrogenated" followed by the ingredient name on the label of certain food packages. Trans fats are present in the majority of margarine brands. They are included to increase the shelf life.

It should be noted, however, that there are natural trans fats. These are the fats produced by the body, and they can also be found in meat and dairy products. Artificial trans fats, according to studies, increase our risk of disease and also cause inflammation.

Trans fats from artificial sources also reduce the amount of good cholesterol (HDL) in the body. According to research, they also impair the endothelial cells that line our arteries, increasing our risk of heart disease.

Certain types of pastries, cookies, French fries, packaged cakes, vegetable shortening, microwave popcorn, margarine, and other types of fast food are commonly cooked with artificial trans fats.

1.6 Foods to Eat

If you already eat a healthy diet, you will have no trouble incorporating these foods into your meals. You may already enjoy them and simply need to make a few changes to make them more prominent in your meal planning. Some of the best foods for preventing and reducing inflammation include:

The following are the most important food types with anti-inflammatory properties.

1. Omega-3 Fatty Acids

Omega-3 fatty acids are found in fish and fish oil. They reassure the white blood cells that they are not in danger of going dormant. Wild salmon and other fish are excellent sources; three times per week is advised. Omega-3 is also found in flax meals and dry beans such as navy beans, kidney beans, and soybeans. If you don't get enough of these foods, an Omega-3 supplement may be beneficial.

2. Fruits and vegetables

Anti-inflammatory properties are found in the majority of fruits and vegetables. They naturally contain antioxidants, carotenoids, lycopene, and magnesium. White blood cell activity has been shown to be significantly reduced by dark green leafy vegetables, as well as colorful fruits and berries.

3. Fats and oils that protect

Yes, there are a few oils and fats that can help people who have inflammation. Among them are coconut oil and extra virgin olive oil. It is also acceptable to consume butter or cream. Ghee is even better because it is free of lactose and casein, which can be problematic if you have lactose intolerance or wheat sensitivity.

4. Fiber

Fiber promotes waste elimination in the body. Because the intestines contain the vast majority of our immune cells, keeping your gut happy is critical. If you don't get enough fiber from your diet, you can take a fiber supplement.

5. Berries

You may be wondering, "Wait a minute, berries are extremely sweet; how can they have an anti-inflammatory effect?" These fruits are also high in antioxidants, fiber, minerals, and vitamins. Fruits in this category include blackberries, raspberries, blueberries, and strawberries. Anthocyanins are antioxidants found in berries. These compounds have anti-inflammatory properties and can significantly reduce the risk of disease transmission. Berries have been shown to boost the number of NK cells in the body when consumed. (natural killer cells). Another study investigates the effects of strawberries on overweight adults. Inflammatory markers associated with cardiovascular disease were found to be significantly lower. There aren't many more compelling reasons to consume berries.

6. Salmon and other Fatty Fish

To fight inflammation effectively, our bodies require a balance of essential fatty acids (omega-six and omega-three fatty acids). Omega-three fatty acids contain anti-inflammatory characteristics, whereas omega-6 fatty acids contain pro-inflammatory characteristics. The ideal omega-6 to omega-three fatty acid ratio, according to functional medicine specialist Chris Kresser, is 1:1 or 2:1.

The challenge is that the typical Western diet is very rich in omega-6 fatty acids, which throws our bodies' ratio out of whack. As a result, the current ratio may be as high as 25:1, indicating that pro-inflammatory fatty acids outnumber anti-inflammatory omega-3 fatty acids significantly. As a result, fish oil supplementation is frequently recommended: It's a stopgap measure to increase omega-3 fatty acids and balance the ratio. While the science surrounding fish oil supplementation is still evolving, it is clear that eating fish is beneficial.

Salmon and other fatty fish (such as herring, mackerel, and tuna) are high in omega-3 fatty acids, which can help your body fight inflammation. Salmon pairs well with greens and citrus fruits, making it simple to create an anti-inflammatory meal with this superstar ingredient.

7. Avocados

Everyone has heard of this superfood, but do you know why it has such a high reputation? Because they contain a lot of monounsaturated fats, fiber, magnesium, and potassium. It contains tocopherols and carotenoids, both of which are known to lower cancer risk. Avocados also contain a chemical compound that can aid in the reduction of inflammation in young skin cells.

8. Green Tea

Green tea is, without a doubt, one of the healthiest beverages you can drink, as it helps to lower your risk of obesity, Alzheimer's disease, heart disease, cancer, and other medical conditions. This beverage contains epigallocatechin-3-gallate, an antioxidant. (also known as EGCG). This substance can reduce inflammation by lowering proinflammatory cytokine production and fatty acid damage.

9. Cinnamon

Cinnamon, a spice that also fights inflammation, has cinnamaldehyde, which inhibits inflammatory agents, according to an article published in the January 2008 issue of Food and Chemical Toxicology.

Cinnamon is suitable for both sweet and savory dishes.

10. Turmeric

With a robust and earthy flavor, this is possibly the most anti-inflammatory spice available. Its fame, however, stems from its high concentration of curcumin, one of the most powerful anti-inflammatory nutrients. This spice can aid in the reduction of inflammation caused by diabetes, arthritis, and other diseases. Consuming just 1 gram of curcumin combined with piperine (from black pepper) can result in a significant decrease in CRP in people suffering from metabolic syndrome. (inflammatory marker). This amount of curcumin may be difficult to obtain from turmeric alone, but taking supplements containing this substance can be extremely beneficial.

11. Garlic

Garlic has long been prized for its anti-inflammatory qualities, which have been supported by scientific research, including one published in the February 2014 issue of Anticancer Agents in Medical Chemistry. Garlic not only fights inflammation but also strengthens the immune system.

Garlic improves the flavor of all plant-based proteins, lean meats, vinaigrettes, and citrus sauces, and it shines when stir-fried with greens or broccoli. It's delicious in chickpea hummus with red bell peppers for dipping.

12. Ginger

Ginger is such an effective anti-inflammatory that it may one day replace NSAIDs as a safer alternative because it inhibits inflammation at the cellular level, according to the Arthritis Foundation's blog. One of the best things about ginger is that it can be used in both sweet and savory dishes. Some of my favorite ways to use it are in chicken soup, and it pairs well with anti-inflammatory fruits like apples and pears.

13. Cocoa and dark chocolate

You can still eat healthily and enjoy the simple pleasures of life. A tasty and satisfying treatment for acute or chronic inflammation. It may surprise you, but the antioxidants in dark chocolate and cocoa have potent anti-inflammatory properties. These ingredients appear to play a role in endothelial cell and artery health. Milk chocolate is not recommended in this case because the anti-inflammatory properties of chocolate require at least 70% cocoa content.

14. Tomatoes

Tomatoes are a nutritional powerhouse due to higher levels of lycopene (an interesting antioxidant with anti-inflammatory properties), potassium, and vitamin C. Lycopene is extremely effective at lowering the levels of proinflammatory chemical compounds linked to cancer. Eat tomatoes in a salad with olive oil to get the most lycopene.

15. Nuts

The fatty acid profile of nuts is the anti-inflammatory secret. Walnuts, macadamias, pecans, almonds, and cashews are your best bets for omega-3 fatty acid-rich nuts.

Nuts can be incorporated into desserts, sprinkled on vegetables, or crushed and used to crust fish or chicken for a delicious anti-inflammatory main course. Nuts are high in calories, so if weight loss is a priority, limit caloric intake to about a handful per day, and rest assured that this level of consumption has been linked to maintaining a healthy weight range.

16. Miscellaneous

Instead of unhealthy fats and oils, eat foods with spices and herbs. Turmeric, cumin, ginger, cloves, and cinnamon are all spices that can help white blood cells relax. Herbs like fennel, rosemary, sage, and thyme can also help decrease inflammation while also adding flavor to your food.

Anti-inflammatory bacteria can be found in fermented foods such as sauerkraut, buttermilk, yogurt, and kimchi.

Healthy snacks include celery, walnuts, carrots, pistachios, almonds, and other vegetables and fruits, as well as unsweetened plain yogurt with fruit mixed in.

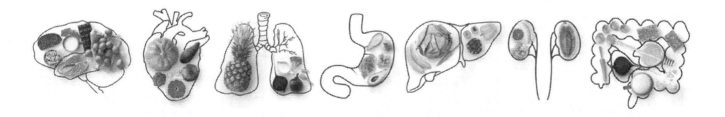

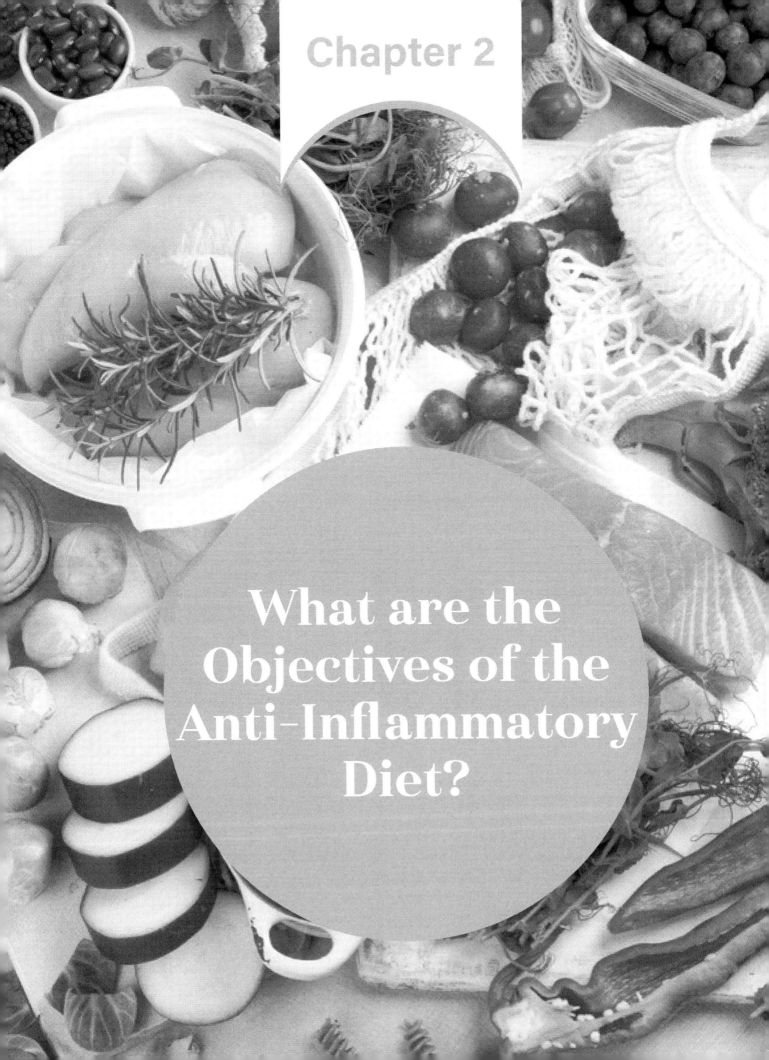

Chapter 2

What are the Objectives of the Anti-Inflammatory Diet?

The objective of the anti-inflammatory diet is to mitigate persistent inflammation in the body, a condition that has been associated with a range of health issues, including but not limited to cardiovascular disease, diabetes, cancer, and Alzheimer's disease. The dietary regimen promotes the intake of complete, nutrient-dense edibles that are abundant in anti-inflammatory agents, such as vitamins, fiber, minerals, and antioxidants. The dietary approach also serves to dissuade the intake of processed and refined foods, alongside those that contain high levels of saturated and trans fats, added sugars, as well as artificial additives, as these have the potential to induce inflammation. The primary objective of the anti-inflammatory diet is to facilitate optimal health and mitigate the likelihood of chronic ailments by bolstering a robust immune system and curbing inflammation within the body.

The anti-inflammatory diet aims to achieve multiple objectives, which include:

2.1 Fertility Enhancement

The role inflammation plays in male and female infertility is largely unknown. Therefore, the best chance of conceiving a child is when inflammation is nonexistent or minimal. Reducing and/or avoiding inflammation during pregnancy reduces the risk of miscarriage and pre-eclampsia. Antioxidants and omega-3 fish oils are beneficial for enhancing fertility and eliminating potential pregnancy complications.

Pre-eclampsia is a condition in which a pregnant woman develops dangerously high blood pressure, endangering both the mother and the unborn child. Pre-eclampsia has been linked to pro-inflammatory cytokines, according to research published in 2018. The University of Mississippi Medical Center was the site of this study. By controlling cytokines, an anti-inflammatory diet lowers the probability of developing pre-eclampsia during pregnancy.

2.2 Reduced Susceptibility to Autoimmune Disorders

Inflammation and autoimmune disorders have occurred together so frequently that the terms can be used interchangeably. While inflammation can be a symptom of autoimmune disease, it can also be a cause. When triggered, the immune system goes into a state of hyper attack, destroying healthy tissue. Lupus, Graves' disease, rheumatoid arthritis, celiac disease, multiple sclerosis, and Addison's disease are just a few of the illnesses that can be brought on by an autoimmune dysfunction.

It stands to reason that a decrease in inflammation would also reduce the risk of developing the aforementioned disorders. It's a mouthful, but it's the correct way to put it. By identifying and modifying a diet that triggers an autoimmune response, inflammation can be prevented.

2.3 Helps Reduce Cancer Risk and May Even Aid in Cancer Treatment

Fruits, vegetables, and whole grains have been shown in numerous studies to lower cancer risk and aid in cancer treatment. However, in order for these foods to have any effect, bad fats and red meat must be avoided. Inflammation causes disorder to reign in sick or damaged cells, a phenomenon most prominent in cancer cells. Instead of attacking and killing off the diseased cells, inflammation serves as a "healing ground" for them. This "healing ground" not only helps them get better but also helps them breed. A healthy anti-inflammatory diet is an effective tool for managing inflammation.

2.4 Optimal Bones Health

Bone-strengthening foods are prevalent in a diet that aims to reduce inflammation. Not all foods have that, but if the anti-inflammatory diet centers on those foods, your bone strength will skyrocket. Bone loss, also known as osteoporosis, can be avoided with the help of anti-inflammatory foods like these.

Find anti-inflammatory foods with a high concentration of phytonutrients if you want robust bone structure. Phytonutrients are plant-based antioxidants that combat free radicals, which have been linked to a number of diseases, including osteoporosis. Examples of phytonutrients include lycopene and beta-carotene.

2.5 Diabetes and metabolic syndrome risk is lowered

High levels of insulin are linked to insulin resistance, which in turn decreases cells' capacity to take in glucose. These are the warning signs of prediabetes, the state before full-blown diabetes sets in. Inflammation brought on by excessive insulin levels makes the situation much worse. When blood sugar and insulin levels are both high, cellular responsiveness decreases. Inflammation raises the risk of glucose dysregulation and insulin resistance.

More research into the link between type 1 and type 2 diabetes and inflammation is needed to combat the disease's prevalence, according to a study published in 2019.

2.6 Lowered Cholesterol Levels

Unfortunately, high cholesterol is not always to blame for CVD. Nonetheless, it should never be disregarded because of how much it increases the danger. Foods that increase triglyceride and blood cholesterol levels are avoided when adopting an anti-inflammatory lifestyle and diet; consequently, anti-inflammatory foods do not have high cholesterol. Inflammatory foods raise not only triglyceride and blood cholesterol levels but also cholesterol levels, in case you were wondering about the link between the two. Don't eat cured meats, fried foods, or any other foods high in inflammatory protein. In order to reduce inflammation and cholesterol levels, eating foods like fruits, whole grains, vegetables, and legumes is highly recommended.

Recent studies have shown that lowering inflammation levels can help lower the risk of cardiovascular disease. The foods themselves are as diverse as the mechanisms they use to lower inflammation and cholesterol. Some foods contain soluble fiber, which aids the body in eliminating cholesterol before it can destroy an important ligament. Some plant-based foods achieve this reduction by lowering levels of bad cholesterol (LDL).

2.7 Sharp Memory

Experts agree that high-sensitivity C-reactive protein (hs-CRP) is an inflammatory marker and that cardiovascular disease impairs human cognitive performance. A link to Alzheimer's disease has also been established.

An inflammatory disease diagnosis is not necessary to begin an anti-inflammatory diet. Even infants and toddlers can benefit from an anti-inflammatory diet. Eight hundred Australian adolescents were studied in 2018, and those who ate a lot of sugary foods, red meat, and processed foods were more likely to develop mental health problems or be overweight as adults. No signs of depression or excess weight were found among the anti-inflammatory diet's adolescent participants. The results of this study were published in Brain, Behavior, and Immunity.

The anti-inflammatory diet's positive effects on cognition last throughout life. Researchers in 2019 found that adhering to a low-inflammatory diet did more than just protect brain tissue; it also greatly reduced neuroinflammation, which is a known risk factor for developing Alzheimer's disease.

2.8 Drop the pounds

Unfortunately, high cholesterol is not always to blame for CVD. Nonetheless, it should never be disregarded because of how much it increases the danger. Foods that increase triglyceride and blood cholesterol levels are avoided when adopting an anti-inflammatory lifestyle and diet; consequently, anti-inflammatory foods do not have high cholesterol. Inflammatory foods raise not only triglyceride and blood cholesterol levels but also cholesterol levels, in case you were wondering about the link between the two. Don't eat cured meats, fried foods, or any other foods high in inflammatory protein. In order to reduce inflammation and cholesterol levels, eating foods like fruits, whole grains, vegetables, and legumes is highly recommended.

Recent studies have shown that lowering inflammation levels can help lower the risk of cardiovascular disease. The foods themselves are as diverse as the mechanisms they use to lower inflammation and cholesterol. Some foods contain soluble fiber, which aids the body in eliminating cholesterol before it can destroy an important ligament. Some plant-based foods achieve this reduction by lowering levels of bad cholesterol (LDL).

2.9 Heart and Blood Vessel Disease Risk is Decreased

For a long time, it was thought that high cholesterol levels caused heart disease, but recent research has shown that inflammation is actually the primary culprit. Cholesterol is simply the body's natural response to the harm inflammation causes.

The highly sensitive cardio C-reactive protein blood test measures the amount of inflammatory substance your body produces. (hsCRP). Anti-inflammatory treatment can reduce the risk of cardiovascular disease when hsCRP levels are elevated.

2.10 Feeling Happier

The inflammatory response is the body's attempt to repair the damage. Still, it becomes a problem and causes discomfort when it gets too long. Pains in the arms and legs, fatigue, difficulty sleeping, and an increased risk of cardiovascular disease and cancer are all symptoms. It's safe to assume that anyone going through all of this is in a foul mood. However, when inflammation is reduced through an anti-inflammatory diet, all the pains and discomfort disappear, and people report feeling better emotionally as a result.

Chapter 3

Which Individuals Tend to Opt for Anti-Inflammatory Diets?

Most experts agree that following an anti-inflammatory diet is a healthy and risk-free choice. However, it may be especially helpful for people who have inflammatory conditions or are at risk for developing chronic diseases. Many people who are either currently dealing with chronic inflammation or would like to avoid ever experiencing it turn to anti-inflammatory diets. Following an anti-inflammatory diet has been shown to reduce inflammation and boost symptoms in people with autoimmune disorders, coronary artery disease, type 2 diabetes, and arthritis. This is due to evidence linking chronic inflammation to the emergence of said conditions.

3.1 Individuals with Inflammatory Problems

Inflammatory bowel disease, rheumatoid arthritis, and other autoimmune disorders are all characterized by inflammation, and patients may find relief by adopting an anti-inflammatory diet. Pain, swelling, and organ damage are all symptoms of the chronic inflammation that characterizes these diseases.

Whole, nutrient-dense foods high in anti-inflammatory vitamins, minerals, and other nutrients are the focus of the anti-inflammatory diet. These foods have been shown to reduce systemic inflammation, which in turn aids in symptom management and general well-being.

Anti-inflammatory diets typically emphasize foods high in anti-inflammatory and oxidative stress-protective antioxidants, such as those found in fruits and vegetables. Healthy fats, like the omega-3 fatty acids found in nuts, fatty fish, and seeds, are emphasized because of their anti-inflammatory effects.

In addition, the anti-inflammatory diet stresses the avoidance of foods like refined carbohydrates, processed foods, and saturated fats, all of which have been linked to increased inflammation.

Overall, people with inflammatory illnesses may find symptom relief and enhanced quality of life by adhering to an anti-inflammatory diet. However, it is crucial to collaborate with a healthcare provider or licensed nutritionist to create a unique anti-inflammatory eating plan that takes into account one's specific requirements.

3.2 Individuals at Risk of Getting Chronic Diseases

An anti-inflammatory diet may be helpful for people who are at risk for developing chronic diseases like type 2 diabetes, heart disease, or cancer. These diseases, along with many others, have been linked to chronic inflammation and its role in their development and progression.

The anti-inflammatory diet emphasizes the consumption of whole, nutrient-dense foods that have been shown to improve health in several different ways, including a decrease in inflammation as well as oxidative stress, maintenance of a balanced gut microbiome, and enhancement of cardiovascular function. These advantages may help lessen the likelihood of contracting chronic illnesses.

Fruits, whole grains, vegetables, and healthy fats are all part of the anti-inflammatory diet because they are high in minerals, vitamins, and other essential nutrients that promote health and well-being. The high fiber content of these foods also aids in controlling blood sugar, lowering cholesterol, and protecting against cardiovascular disease and type 2 diabetes.

In addition, the anti-inflammatory diet stresses the avoidance of foods like refined carbohydrates, processed foods, and saturated fats, all of which have been linked to increased inflammation. There is mounting evidence that consumption of these foods contributes to chronic inflammation and disease.

People who are at risk for developing chronic diseases may be able to lower their risk and improve their health and well-being by adopting an anti-inflammatory diet. However, it is crucial to collaborate with a healthcare provider or registered dietitian to create a unique anti-inflammatory eating plan that takes into account one's specific requirements.

3.3 Those Looking to Drop Pounds

Those on a mission to trim down might also benefit from adhering to an anti-inflammatory eating plan. The plan emphasizes unprocessed, nutrient-rich foods that are also low in added sugars as well as unhealthy fats, which can aid in calorie restriction and weight loss.

Fruits, whole grains, vegetables, and legumes are highlighted on the anti-inflammatory diet because they are high in fiber and can make you feel fuller for longer. This can aid in controlling portions and facilitating the maintenance of a healthy diet.

Not only is weight loss, not the main objective of the anti-inflammatory diet, but the amount of weight one loses also depends on variables such as one's starting weight, level of physical activity, and general health. Working with a healthcare provider or registered dietitian to create a personalized weight loss plan which includes anti-inflammatory principles may be helpful if weight loss is the primary goal.

3.4 Whoever Wants to Maintain their Fitness and Eat Healthily

If you want to eat healthily and exercise regularly, an anti-inflammatory diet may be the way to go. Foods that are high in vitamins, minerals, fiber, and antioxidants, take center stage in the diet.

The anti-inflammatory diet, which emphasizes these foods, has been shown to improve health and well-being and to aid in maintaining a healthy weight. Omega-3 fatty acids, which can be found in foods like flaxseeds, fatty fish, and walnuts, are also encouraged by the diet. The anti-inflammatory and cardio-protective properties of these healthy fats are well-documented.

The anti-inflammatory diet, taken as a whole, is a healthy and nutritious eating plan that is beneficial for people of all ages and physical abilities. It should be noted, however, that the diet is not a cookie-cutter solution and may need to be adjusted to fit the specific requirements of the individual. A personalized anti-inflammatory eating plan can be created with the help of a registered dietitian.

3.5 Those Who Wish to Extend Their Lifespan

Individuals who want to live longer may also benefit from adopting an anti-inflammatory eating pattern. The diet emphasizes nutrient-dense, whole foods low in unhealthy fats, added sugars, and processed foods, which can all contribute to chronic disease and inflammation in the body as a whole.

The anti-inflammatory diet has been shown to reduce the risk of chronic diseases like heart disease, type 2 diabetes, cancer, and Alzheimer's by improving overall health and lowering the body's inflammatory response. Individuals may be able to enhance their health and longevity by reducing the inflammation that contributes to these conditions through dietary and behavioral changes.

Vegetables, fruits, seeds, nuts, and whole grains are all recommended as part of the anti-inflammatory diet because of their high levels of antioxidants along with additional anti-inflammatory compounds. These foods have been shown to have anti-aging and disease-fighting properties by protecting against free radicals and other toxic compounds in the body.

Even though the anti-inflammatory diet has been shown to have positive effects on longevity and health, it's important to remember that other lifestyle factors, such as stress management, regular exercise, and adequate sleep, are also crucial.

4.3 Vegan or Vegetarian Diet

A vegan or vegetarian diet is one that does not include any animal products in any way, shape, or form, including meat, dairy, or eggs. Fruits, vegetables, nuts, legumes, whole grains, and seeds are all examples of nutrient-dense, whole foods that can be included in these diets for their potential anti-inflammatory effects.

4.4 Whole Food Diet

A whole-food diet is one that emphasizes unprocessed foods and limits or eliminates the consumption of refined carbohydrates, added sugars, and fats that are unhealthy. Fruits, vegetables, nuts, legumes, whole grains, and seeds are all part of this diet.

4.5 Plant-based Diet

Unlike strict vegan or vegetarian regimens, a plant-based diet allows for the occasional consumption of fish, eggs, and dairy. Fruits, vegetables, whole grains, nuts, legumes, and seeds take center stage, while refined carbohydrates, unhealthy fats, and processed foods are restricted or avoided altogether.

When it comes to anti-inflammatory diets, the Mediterranean diet has been studied the most. The DASH eating plan comes in second. Inflammation can be fought with even a vegan or vegetarian diet. Whole plant-based foods, whole wheat, healthy fats, and moderate amounts of animal protein are the cornerstones of a healthy diet.

The anti-inflammatory effects of an anti-inflammatory diet are the result of the synergistic effects of the diet's individual components. Lifestyle changes are emphasized in the anti-inflammatory Mediterranean diet and other similar eating plans for optimal health benefits.

If the scope of the necessary adjustments seems too great, start small. This will increase the likelihood that your new habits will become permanent rather than a passing fad. Eating well is just as important as making healthy lifestyle choices like managing stress, making time for loved ones, getting regular exercise, and getting enough sleep.

The anti-inflammatory effects of these diets have not been firmly established, and the particulars of each diet may vary depending on the needs and health conditions of the individual. If you want to know what anti-inflammatory diet is best for you, talk to your doctor or a registered dietitian.

RECIPES

Chapter 5: Breakfast Recipes

1. Cauli Avocado Toast

Preparation time: 10 minutes | **Cooking time:** 20 minutes | **Servings:** 2

Nutritional Value: Calories 278 | Total Fat 15.6g | Protein 14.1g | Carbs 7.7g

Ingredients:

- 1/2 teaspoon of garlic powder
- 1 avocado ripe
- 2 tablespoons of olive oil extra virgin
- 1 cup of crumbled feta cheese
- 12 oz. of steamer bag cauliflower
- 1/4 teaspoon of black pepper
- 1 egg large

Instructions:

- Cauliflower should be prepared according to package directions, and any excess water should be wrung out using a kitchen towel or cheesecloth.
- Warm the olive oil inside a medium, nonstick skillet over medium flame. Separate the cauliflower mixture into two mounds on the baking paper. Create a 1/4-inch-wide by 1-inch-long rectangle by pressing the peaks together.
- For about 8 minutes in a skillet, they will be ready. After you've flipped the cauliflower, cook it for another 4 minutes. When you're done, put it away to cool for a while.
- After slicing the avocado in half lengthwise and removing the pit, mash the flesh in a medium-sized mixing bowl with the pepper and garlic powder. Coat the cauliflower with the sauce and serve!

2. Fluffy Courgette Omelet

Preparation time: 10 minutes | **Cooking time:** 20 minutes | **Servings:** 1

Nutritional Value: Calories 350 | Total Fat 27.6g | Protein 21.1g | Carbs 3.3g

Ingredients:

- 2 eggs separated
- 1 to 2 tablespoons of Olive oil
- 1 tablespoon of parmesan cheese grated
- Salt and pepper to taste
- 2 finely chopped spring onions
- 1 medium grated courgette
- Butter

Instructions:

- Cook the courgette for three to four minutes in the olive oil inside a medium-sized skillet over medium flame, then add the spring onion and cook for another minute. Take them out of the flame and put them somewhere else.

- In two different bowls, use an electric mixer to whip the egg whites until stiff, and then beat the egg yolks with 1 tablespoon of water. Add some salt and pepper to the egg whites and the yolks to taste.

- Olive oil should be heated in a skillet large enough to hold the eggs; add the eggs, and the sautéed courgette and spring onions should be pressed down on top. The eggs would benefit from a sprinkling of parmesan.

- Cook for about 10 minutes, turning the eggs over once.

3. Summer Fruit Compote with Honeyed Greek Yogurt

Preparation time: 10 minutes | **Cooking time:** 20 minutes | **Servings:** 4

Nutritional Value: Calories 167 | Total Fat 1g | Protein 2g | Carbs 11g

Ingredients:

- 1 teaspoon of ground cinnamon
- 2 cups of red wine like Merlot
- 1 teaspoon of vanilla extract
- 1 lb. of pitted, halved, and thinly sliced peaches
- Quality honey to your liking
- 1 lb. of halved and pitted cherries
- 3/4 cup of cane sugar
- 1 1/2 cup of Greek yogurt plain(fat-free)

Instructions:

- Combine sliced peaches and cherries in a large-sized mixing bowl. On top,

sprinkle using cinnamon. Toss them together. Place them aside.

- Combine the sugar and wine inside a saucepan. Warm for 5 minutes on high till the sugar is completely dissolved.

- Pour the hot wine syrup over the fruit. Cover and set aside for about 1 hour to cool. The syrup should be discarded in large quantities, but some of it should be saved in a cup for later use.

- Inside a small-sized cup, combine the honey, Greek yogurt, and vanilla extract. Stir. Serve the poached fruit with honeyed Greek yogurt and a drizzle of poaching syrup.

4. Apple Muffins

Preparation time: 10 minutes | **Cooking time:** 25 minutes | **Servings:** 12 muffins

Nutritional Value: Calories 76 | Total Fat 1g | Protein 3g | Carbs 15g

Ingredients:

- 2 cups of rolled oats
- Pinch of kosher salt
- 4 medium egg whites
- 2 teaspoons of cinnamon
- 1 peeled and diced apple
- 2 scoops of vanilla protein powder
- 1/2 teaspoon of baking powder
- 2 tablespoons of sugar substitute
- 1 cup of non-fat Greek yogurt

Instructions:

- Preheat the oven to 350°F and lightly spray a 12-muffin baking pan with cooking spray.

- Combine all of the ingredients inside a large-sized mixing bowl and stir well. Distribute evenly among muffin cups till everything is mixed.
- Bake for around 15 to 20 minutes at 350°F. Allow to cool completely before serving.

5. Hash Potatoes with Poached Eggs

Preparation time: 10 minutes | **Cooking time:** 20 minutes | **Servings:** 4

Nutritional Value: Calories 535 | Total Fat 20.8g | Protein 26.6g | Carbs 34.5g

Ingredients:

- 1 lb. of baby asparagus, discard the hard ends and chop them into one-fourth-inch pieces
- 2 cloves of chopped garlic
- 1 teaspoon of dried oregano
- Pinch of sweetener
- Salt and pepper
- 1 finely chopped small red onion
- 1/2 cup of crumbled feta
- Extra virgin olive oil
- 1 finely chopped small yellow onion
- 1 teaspoon of coriander
- 2 diced russet potatoes
- 1 teaspoon of white vinegar
- 1 1/2 teaspoons of ground allspice
- 1 cup of chickpeas
- Water
- 1 teaspoon of Za'atar

- 4 poached eggs
- 1 teaspoon of smoked paprika
- 2 chopped Roma tomatoes
- 1 cup of fresh parsley chopped

Instructions:

- Inside a large-sized cast-iron skillet, heat 1/2 tablespoon of olive oil. In a skillet, heat the garlic, onions, and potatoes over medium-high flame. Season to taste using salt and pepper. Cook for 5-7 minutes, stirring frequently, or till the potatoes are soft.
- Add the asparagus, chickpeas, spices, and a pinch of salt and pepper to taste. Stir everything together to combine. Cook for an additional 5-7 minutes. To keep the potato hash warm, reduce the flame to low and stir frequently.
- Meanwhile, bring 1 teaspoon of vinegar to a steady simmer inside a medium-sized pot of water. Fill a mug halfway with eggs. Place the eggs in the simmering water after gently stirring them. The egg whites can warp as they wrap around the yoke. Cook for 3 minutes, then remove the eggs from the water and drain them with a kitchen towel. Season using salt and pepper to taste.
- Remove from the flame and top with the tomatoes, crumbled feta, and parsley. Set the poached eggs on top.

6. Green Shakshuka

Preparation time: 10 minutes | **Cooking time:** 25 minutes | **Servings:** 4

Nutritional Value: Calories 229.6 | Total Fat 18.2g | Protein 9g | Carbs 9.8g

Ingredients:

- 1/2 finely chopped red onion large
- Kosher salt
- 2 cups of baby spinach (around 2.5 ounces)
- A handful of fresh parsley for garnishing
- 8 ounces of trimmed and sliced Brussels sprouts
- 3/4 teaspoon of cumin
- 1 teaspoon of coriander
- 1/2 lemon juice
- 1 bunch of large kale (around 8 ounces) chopped and thick veins discarded
- 1/4 cup of olive oil
- 1 teaspoon of Aleppo pepper
- 3 cloves of minced garlic
- 1 trimmed and chopped green onion
- 4 eggs large
- Feta cheese crumbled for garnish

Instructions:

- Warm the olive oil inside a covered 10-inch skillet over a medium-high flame until it shimmers but does not burn. Season using kosher salt to taste after adding the sliced Brussels sprouts. Cook, tossing occasionally, for 5-6 minutes or till softened and color develops.
- Turn the flame down to medium. Cook for 3 to 4 minutes, tossing frequently, or until the garlic and onions are softened (don't let the garlic burn; adjust the heat as needed).
- Cook for 5 minutes or till the kale wilts slightly. Thoroughly

incorporate the spinach. Add a tablespoon of kosher salt to taste.

- Mix in the spices thoroughly. Add half a cup of water. Reduce the flame to a low setting. Cook, covered, for around 8 to 10 minutes or till the kale is fully wilted. Thoroughly incorporate the lemon juice.
- Make four wells using a spoon. Fill each well with an egg and season using salt. Cook for 4 minutes more, covered, till the eggs are done to your liking.
- Turn off the flame. If desired, drizzle with more extra virgin olive oil. Serve garnished with parsley, green onions, and a dollop of creamy feta cheese. Serve right away with warm pita bread or your favorite whole-wheat bread.

7. Caprese Stuffed Avocado

Preparation time: 10 minutes | **Cooking time:** 20 minutes | **Servings:** 4

Nutritional Value: Calories 191 | Total Fat 16g | Protein 5g | Carbs 10g

Ingredients:

- 2/3 cup of grape tomatoes halved
- Sea salt
- 4 teaspoons of balsamic vinegar
- Black pepper
- 2 oz. of fresh mozzarella cheese (cut into small pieces)
- 1/4 cup of fresh basil
- 2 California avocado large

Instructions:

- Preheat the oven to 350°F.

- Remove the pits from the avocados and cut them in half. Set aside half of the flesh from each avocado and set the other half aside.

- Mash avocados using a fork in a medium-sized mixing bowl. Combine fresh mozzarella, grape tomatoes, and fresh basil. Combine the black pepper and sea salt.

- Fill the avocado halves with the mixture, and place them on a baking sheet.

- Bake for 10 to 12 minutes before serving.

8. Egg in an Avocado Boat

Preparation time: 10 minutes | **Cooking time:** 20 minutes | **Servings:** 2

Nutritional Value: Calories 280 | Total Fat 23.5g | Protein 11.3g | Carbs 9.3g

Ingredients:

- 2 medium-size eggs
- 1 avocado halved and pitted
- 2 teaspoons of fresh chives chopped
- Pinch of black pepper and sea salt
- 2 slices of bacon cooked and crumbled

Instructions:

- Preheat the oven to 380°F.
- Fill a small-sized cup halfway with two eggs, being careful not to break the yolks. Make certain that the eggs are not broken.
- Half an avocado should be placed on a baking sheet. 1 egg yolk should be placed gently in each half-avocado hole. Fill the cavity with egg white till it is completely full. Proceed in the same manner with the remaining avocado. Each avocado should be topped with chives, salt, and pepper.

- Bake for around 10 to 15 minutes, depending on the size of the pan.

9. Cauliflower Hash Browns

Preparation time: 10 minutes | **Cooking time:** 15 minutes | **Servings:** 4

Nutritional Value: Calories 153 | Total Fat 9.5g | Protein 10.0g | Carbs 3.0g

Ingredients:

- 2 tablespoons of olive oil extra virgin
- 1 cup of skim-part grated parmesan cheese
- 2 oz. of steamer bag cauliflower
- 1 large egg

Instructions:

- Microwave a cauliflower bag according to the package directions. Cool the cauliflower in a kitchen towel or cheesecloth. Squeeze the bottle tightly to remove any remaining moisture.

- Mash cauliflower with a fork, then add cheese and egg.

- Heat the oil inside a large-sized nonstick skillet over a medium flame. Place each hash brown patty in the skillet with 1/4 of the mixture.

- Cook on a medium flame for 12 minutes. Flip the hash browns halfway through cooking time. Cook until golden brown on both sides. Serve immediately.

10. Granola with Olive Oil

Preparation time: 10 minutes | **Cooking time:** 30 minutes | **Servings:** 14

Nutritional Value: Calories 392 | Total Fat 1.6g | Protein 8.1g | Carbs 40.1g

Ingredients:

- 3/4 cup of walnuts
- 2 teaspoons of vanilla extract pure
- 1 cup of coconut flakes unsweetened
- 2/3 cup of tahini
- 1/2 teaspoon of ground cinnamon
- 1/2 cup of dried cranberries
- 3/4 cup of shelled pistachios
- 1/3 cup of light brown sugar packed
- 2 1/2 cups of old-fashioned rolled oats
- 1/2 cup of Medjool dates chopped
- 1/2 cup of sunflower seed
- 3/4 cup of warmed-up honey
- 1/2 cup of olive oil
- 3 tablespoons of sesame seeds raw
- 1/2 teaspoon of cardamom

Instructions:

- Preheat the oven to 400°F.
- Inside a large-sized mixing bowl, combine the oats, sesame seeds, walnuts, sunflower seeds, pistachios, and coconut flakes.
- Combine the tahini, honey, olive oil, cinnamon, vanilla extract, brown sugar, and cardamom in a separate bowl. Toss the oat mixture with the spread to coat evenly.
- Spread the mixture in a single layer on a large sheet pan. Bake for 20 minutes, stirring every 5 minutes, till the bread is well-toasted and golden.
- Allow the granola to cool completely. Mix in the dates and cranberries after they have been broken up into clusters.

11. Taleggio Mushroom Omelet

Preparation time: 10 minutes | **Cooking time:** 15 minutes | **Servings:** 2

Nutritional Value: Calories 396 | Total Fat 31.4g | Protein 27.1g | Carbs 0.8g

Ingredients:

- 50g of taleggio sliced
- 2 teaspoons of olive oil
- 150g of chestnut mushrooms sliced
- A handful of rocket leaves
- 2 eggs seasoned and beaten
- 1 crushed garlic clove

Instructions:

- Inside a medium-sized nonstick frying pan, heat the olive oil.
- Inside a mixing bowl, combine all of the above ingredients and spread the batter in a frying pan.
- Cook for about 10–12 minutes, flipping halfway through.

12. Turkish Scrambled Eggs with Tomatoes

Preparation time: 10 minutes | **Cooking time:** 20 minutes | **Servings:** 4

Nutritional Value: Calories 164.7 | Total Fat 11.5g | Protein 7.2g | Carbs 9.3g

Ingredients:

- 1 chopped medium yellow onion
- 2 tablespoons of extra virgin olive oil
- Black pepper
- 2 tomatoes vine-ripe
- 1/2 teaspoon of dried oregano
- Pinch of red pepper flakes crushed
- 1 seeded, cored, and chopped green bell pepper
- Kosher salt
- 1 teaspoon of Aleppo pepper
- 3 tablespoons of tomato paste
- 1 French baguette for serving (optional)
- 4 beaten large eggs

Instructions:

- In a 10-inch skillet, melt 2 tablespoons butter over medium flame. Combine the onions, kosher salt, and peppers. Cook for 4 to 5 minutes, stirring frequently, or till softened.
- Combine the tomato paste and tomatoes. Season using kosher salt, black pepper, oregano, and Aleppo pepper to taste. Cook for a few minutes more over medium flame, stirring occasionally, until the tomatoes soften.
- Place the pepper and tomato mixture in one of the pan's corners. Reduce the flame to medium-low. Pour in the beaten egg and cook, stirring gently as needed, until the eggs are just set.
- Drizzle with olive oil and season to taste with Aleppo pepper and red pepper flakes. Serve with thick slices of bread right away.

13. Vegetable Frittata

Preparation time: 10 minutes | **Cooking time:** 20 minutes | **Servings:** 4

Nutritional Value: Calories 168 | Total Fat 11.8g | Protein 10.2g | Carbs 6.5g

Ingredients:

- 1/4 cup of heavy whipping cream
- 1/2 cup of grape tomatoes
- Salt and pepper according to taste
- 1/4 cup of green bell pepper chopped
- 1/2 cup of chopped spinach
- 6 large size eggs
- 1/2 cup of chopped broccoli
- 1/4 cup of yellow onion chopped

Instructions:

- Preheat the oven to 350°F.
- Inside a large-sized mixing bowl, whisk together whipping cream and eggs. Combine the spinach, onion, tomatoes, bell pepper, and broccoli.
- Bake for approximately 30 minutes in a 6-inch greased round oven-safe baking dish.

- In a preheated oven, bake for 12 to 15 minutes.

14. Breakfast Shake

Preparation time: 5 minutes | **Cooking time:** 0 minutes | **Servings:** 3 cups

Nutritional Value: Calories 299 | Total Fat 12.4g | Protein 5.7g | Carbs 47.7g

Ingredients:

- 1/4 cup of crushed ice
- 4 medium Medjool dates pitted
- 1/4 cup of tahini
- 1 1/2 cups of almond milk unsweetened
- 2 frozen bananas chunks
- Pinch of ground cinnamon

Instructions:

- In a mixer, combine the frozen banana chunks and the remaining ingredients. Blend till you have a thick, creamy shake.
- Pour the shake into serving glasses and top with ground cinnamon.

15. Chicken and Veggie Omelet

Preparation time: 10 minutes | **Cooking time:** 25 minutes | **Servings:** 6

Nutritional Value: Calories 200 | Total Fat 10g | Protein 19g | Carbs 7g

Ingredients:

- 1/4 cup of plain Greek yogurt fat-free
- 1 teaspoon of Dijon mustard
- 4 cups of baby spinach
- 8 medium eggs
- 1 cup of grated carrots
- 3 tablespoons of olive oil
- 1/3 teaspoon of salt
- 3 tablespoons of asiago cheese grated
- 1/2 lb. of chicken breasts, skinless and boneless
- 1 cup of red onions sliced

Instructions:

- Cut the chicken breasts into 1/2-inch strips.
- Heat 1 teaspoon olive oil inside a medium-sized pan and cook the chicken breasts with the onions for around 10 minutes or till golden brown. Transfer to a plate and return to the pan using the remaining olive oil.
- In a mixing bowl, whisk together the eggs, Dijon mustard, and salt till well combined. Fill the nonstick skillet halfway with the mixture. Sprinkle the egg mixture, cooked chicken, and onion with the grated spinach and carrot. Incorporate the spinach into the mixture.
- Cook for approximately 15 minutes, flipping halfway through. Top with Asiago cheese and cut into six slices. Serve with a green salad to round out the meal.

Chapter 6: Vegetarian and Vegan

1. Zucchini with Rice and Tzatziki

Preparation time: 15 minutes | **Cooking time:** 35 minutes | **Servings:** 4

Nutritional Value: Calories: 414 | Fat: 17g | Carbohydrates: 47g | Protein: 5g

Ingredients:

- 1 cup of short-grain brown rice
- ¼ cup of olive oil
- 3 zucchinis, diced
- 1 cup of Tzatziki sauce
- Freshly ground black pepper
- 1 cup of vegetable broth
- Salt

- 2 tablespoons of pine nuts
- 1 chopped onion
- ½ cup of chopped fresh dill

Instructions:

- Inside a heavy-bottomed pot, heat the oil over a medium flame. Cook for about 5 minutes on medium-low flame, stirring occasionally. Cook for another 2 minutes after adding the zucchini.

- Season using salt and pepper after adding the vegetable broth and dill. Turn the flame up to medium and bring the mixture to a boil.

- Return the mixture to a boil after adding the rice. Reduce the flame to low, cover, and leave to cook for around 15 to 20 minutes. Remove from the flame and leave to cool for 10 minutes. Serve with tzatziki sauce and a scoop of rice on a serving dish topped with pine nuts.

2. Roasted Vegetable Barley

Preparation time: 10 minutes | **Cooking time:** 40 minutes | **Servings:** 6

Nutritional Value: Calories: 192 | Fat: 5g | Carbohydrates: 33g | Protein: 5g

Ingredients:

- 2 diced zucchini squash
- ¾ teaspoon of smoked paprika
- Feta cheese
- 1 diced red onion
- Olive oil
- 1 minced garlic clove
- Water

- 1 cup of pearl barley
- 2 teaspoons of harissa spice
- Black pepper to taste
- 2 tablespoons of lemon juice
- 1 diced bell pepper (red & yellow)
- Salt to taste
- 4 tablespoons of chopped parsley
- Toasted pine nuts
- 2 chopped scallions

Instructions:

- Boil the barley in water for 45 minutes.
- Combine the pepper, veggies, salt, harissa spice, paprika, and oil inside a mixing bowl.
- Roast for around 25 minutes at 425°F in a preheated oven.
- Inside a large-sized mixing bowl, combine the roasted vegetables, cooked barley, scallions, lemon juice, parsley, garlic, and oil. To coat, toss well.

3. Greens Tacos with Chickpeas & Turnips

Preparation time: 10 minutes | **Cooking time:** 0 minutes | **Servings:** 12

Nutritional Value: Calories: 257 | Fat: 8g | Carbohydrates: 39g | Protein: 9g

Ingredients:

- 1 tablespoon of lemon juice
- 12 corn tortillas
- ½ tablespoon of olive oil

- 1 cup of chickpeas
- 1 minced garlic
- 1/4 cup of crumbled Feta cheese
- 1 tablespoon of chopped parsley
- 1 1/4 cups of turnip greens
- 1 minced red onion
- Black pepper
- 1 shredded cucumber
- ¼ teaspoon of sea salt

Instructions:

- Inside a large-sized mixing bowl, combine the garlic, onions, and chickpeas.
- Season using salt and pepper to taste.
- Mix in the parsley, olive oil, and lemon juice.
- Mix till the mixture resembles a thick paste.
- Add the frozen turnip greens. Mix.
- Spread some chickpea turnip greens batter on a warmed corn tortilla. (in a skillet or the oven, if you like).
- Garnish with feta cheese and cucumber slices. Enjoy!

4. Cucumber and Olive Rice

Preparation time: 55 minutes | **Cooking time:** 15 minutes | **Servings:** 8

Nutritional Value: Calories: 223 | Fat: 13g | Carbohydrates: 24g | Protein: 5g

Ingredients:

- 1.5 cups of brown rice
- 1 cup of parsley leaves

- Black pepper to taste
- 3 chopped cucumbers
- 1 lb. of heirloom
- 3 garlic cloves
- Kosher salt to taste
- 1 cup of feta
- 7 tablespoons of olive oil
- 1 chopped onion
- 3 tablespoons of sherry vinegar
- 1 cup of mint leaves

Instructions:

- In a hot frying pan, add 2 tablespoons of oil.
- Cook for another five minutes after adding the garlic and salt. Cook, constantly stirring, till the mixture is fragrant and translucent. Place this in a mixing bowl.
- Return the frying pan to the flame and add the rice and 1 tablespoon of oil. Cook, stirring constantly, for about three minutes or till the mixture is brown and nutty.
- Bring a half-full dish of water to a boil. Mix it only once, then reduce the flame to low and cover it. Cook until the rice is tender and the water has been absorbed. Remove it from the flame and set it aside to cool for about five minutes.
- Set aside the rice and onion mixture in a bowl for 20 minutes to cool.
- Combine the vinegar, tomatoes, cucumbers, and the remaining oil inside a mixing bowl. To taste, season with black pepper and sea salt.
- Finally, garnish with the cheese, parsley, and mint.

5. Pumpkin, Cauliflower, and Chickpeas Curry

Preparation time: 10 minutes | **Cooking time:** 25 minutes | **Servings:** 4

Nutritional Value: Calories: 263 | Fat: 2g | Carbohydrates: 44g | Protein: 12g

Ingredients:

- 1 tablespoon of oil
- 2 cups of cauliflower florets
- 1 sliced onion
- 2 cups of butternut pumpkin
- 1 teaspoon of cumin powder
- 1 tomato diced
- 1/2 teaspoon of turmeric
- 1 teaspoon of chili powder
- 1 cup of chickpeas boiled
- Salt
- 1 tablespoon of coriander powder
- Curry Powder

Instructions:

- In a pot, combine the onions, diced pumpkin, and tomato, as well as one cup of water. It's been pressure cooked for about 6 minutes now. Allow pressure to escape naturally. In a blender, combine all of the ingredients.
- In a pot, combine the oil and cauliflower and cook for about 15 minutes or till golden brown.
- Before adding the Puree and bringing it to a boil, stir in the cooked chickpeas and curry powder. Season using salt and pepper to taste.

- Serve immediately with rice.

6. Asparagus Risotto

Preparation time: 15 minutes | **Cooking time:** 30 minutes | **Servings:** 4

Nutritional Value: Calories: 434 | Fat: 14g | Carbohydrates: 57g | Protein: 6g

Ingredients:

- 1 tablespoon of olive oil
- 1 small chopped onion
- 5 cups of vegetable broth divided
- 1½ cups of Arborio rice
- 3 tablespoons of unsalted butter, divided
- 1-pound of fresh asparagus ends trimmed, cut into one-inch pieces, & tips separated
- ¼ cup of grated Parmesan cheese

Instructions:

- Over medium flame, bring the vegetable broth to a boil. Reduce the flame to low and allow it to simmer. Mix in 2 tablespoons of melted butter and 2 teaspoons of olive oil. Cook for 2 to 3 minutes after adding the onion.
- Stir the rice in the pan for 1 minute or till it is completely coated with oil and butter.
- Add 1/2 cup of hot broth. Cook, stirring constantly, until the broth is completely absorbed. Add the asparagus stalks and the remaining 1/2 cup of broth. Cook, stirring constantly. Continue to add the broth in 1/2 cup increments, heating until the previous 1/2 cup has been absorbed completely before adding the next 1/2 cup. To prevent sticking, stir frequently. Rice should be soft but firm when cooked.
- Combine the asparagus tips, 1 tablespoon of butter, and the Parmesan cheese. To combine, vigorously stir everything together. Remove from the flame, sprinkle with additional Parmesan cheese, and serve immediately.

7. Arugula Salad with Figs and Walnuts

Preparation time: 15 minutes | **Cooking time:** 10 minutes | **Servings:** 2

Nutritional Value: Calories: 403 | Fat: 9g | Carbohydrates: 35g | Protein: 13g

Ingredients:

- 3 tablespoons of olive oil
- ½ cup of dried figs, cut into wedges
- 1 can of salt-free chickpeas, drained
- 5 oz. of arugula
- 1/2 cup of goat cheese, crumbled
- 2 teaspoons of balsamic vinegar
- 1 teaspoon of honey
- 1 carrot, scraped
- Salt, to taste
- 1/8 teaspoon of cayenne pepper
- ½ walnuts, cut in half

Instructions:

- Preheat the oven to 175°F. Combine the nuts, cayenne pepper, 1 tablespoon olive oil, and 1/8 teaspoon salt inside a baking dish.

Place the baking sheet in the oven and roast the nuts until they are golden brown. When you're finished, set it aside.

- Combine the honey, 2 tablespoons of oil, balsamic vinegar, and 3/4 teaspoon of salt inside a mixing bowl.

- Toss the arugula, carrots, and figs together in a large-sized mixing bowl. Dress the nuts and goat cheese with the balsamic honey vinaigrette. Check that you have covered everything.

8. Loaded Chickpeas Bowls

Preparation time: 10 minutes | **Cooking time:** 10 minutes | **Servings:** 6

Nutritional Value: Calories: 308 | Fat: 15g | Carbohydrates: 17g | Protein: 11g

Ingredients:

- Salt to taste
- 1 cup of chopped dill
- 3 tablespoons of Za'atar spice
- 1 cup of cooked chickpeas
- Olive oil
- 1 sliced eggplant
- ½ chopped English cucumber
- 1 chopped small red onion
- 3 diced Roma tomatoes
- 1 cup of chopped parsley

Garlic Vinaigrette:

- 1/3 cup of extra virgin olive oil
- 2 chopped garlic cloves

- Salt to taste
- 2 tablespoons of lime juice
- Black pepper to taste

Instructions:

- Set aside for 30 minutes after salting the eggplant.
- Cook eggplant for 5 minutes on each side in olive oil.
- Remove the eggplant from the skillet when it has turned brown on all sides and set it aside.
- In a mixing bowl, combine cucumber, onions, zaatar, chickpeas, tomatoes, dill, and parsley.
- Combine all of the dressing ingredients in a mixing bowl.
- Pour the dressing over the cooked eggplant and chickpeas in a large mixing bowl.
- Serve right away and enjoy.

9. Roasted Italian Vegetables

Preparation time: 10 minutes | **Cooking time:** 30 minutes | **Servings:** 6

Nutritional Value: Calories: 88 | Fat: 1g | Carbohydrates: 14g | Protein: 4g

Ingredients:

- 1 1/4 cups of Campari tomatoes
- 2 sliced zucchinis
- Red pepper flakes to taste
- 1 cup of mushrooms
- Shredded Parmesan cheese
- ½ tablespoon of dried oregano

- 1 chopped garlic cloves
- Salt to taste
- 1 1/2 cups of sliced baby potatoes
- Extra virgin olive, as required
- 1 teaspoon of dried thyme
- Black pepper to taste

Instructions:

- Combine the salt, mushrooms, garlic, olive oil, pepper, vegetables, oregano, and thyme in a mixing bowl. Set aside for the time being.
- In a preheated oven, bake potatoes for about 10 minutes at 425°F.
- Bake for another 20 minutes after combining the mushroom mixture with the baked potatoes.
- Garnish with cheese and pepper flakes if desired.

10. Moroccan Couscous with Chickpeas

Preparation time: 10 minutes | **Cooking time:** 20 minutes | **Servings:** 6

Nutritional Value: Calories: 649 | Fat: 14g | Carbohydrates: 60g | Protein: 30g

Ingredients:

- ¼ cup of olive oil, extra for serving
- 2 peeled & chopped fine carrots
- ¼ teaspoon of ground anise seed
- 1 (15-ounces) can of rinsed chickpeas
- 1 ½ cups of frozen peas
- 3 cloves of garlic minced

- 1 teaspoon of ground ginger
- Lemon wedges
- 1 ½ cups of couscous
- 1 teaspoon of ground coriander
- 1 ¾ cups of chicken broth
- Salt & pepper
- 1 chopped fine onion
- ½ cup of chopped fresh parsley

Instructions:

- In a skillet, heat 2 tablespoons of oil over medium flame. Cook for 3 to 5 minutes or till the couscous starts to brown. To clean the skillet, place it in a bowl.
- In the same skillet, heat the remaining 2 tablespoons of oil and add the carrots, onion, and 1 teaspoon of salt. Cook for about 5 to 7 minutes. Incorporate the anise, coriander, ginger, and garlic. Cook till the mixture smells good. (about 30 seconds).
- Bring the chickpeas and broth to a boil in a saucepan. Combine the couscous and peas in a mixing bowl. Cover the pan and turn off the flame. Remove from the flame and allow to cool until the couscous is tender.
- After tossing the parsley with the couscous, mash it with a fork and season with a dash of extra oil and a generous pinch of salt and pepper. Serve with lemon slices on the side.

11. Kale, Quinoa & Avocado Salad with Lemon Dijon Vinaigrette

Preparation time: 5 minutes | **Cooking time:** 25 minutes | **Servings:** 4

Nutritional Value: Calories: 342 | Fat: 20g | Carbohydrates: 35g | Protein: 9g

Ingredients:

- 1/2 cup of chopped cucumber
- 2/3 cup of quinoa
- 1 bunch of kale torn into bite-sized pieces
- 2 tablespoons of chopped red onion
- 1 1/3 cups of water
- 1 tablespoon of feta crumbled
- 1/3 cup of chopped red pepper
- 1/2 avocado - peeled, diced & pitted

Instructions:

- Inside a saucepan, bring the quinoa and 1 1/3 cups of water to a boil. Reduce the flame to low and continue to cook for 15 to 20 minutes till the quinoa is soft, and the water is absorbed. Allow to cool completely before serving.
- Put the cabbage in a steam basket in a pan with at least an inch of boiling hot water. Close the lid and steam for 45 seconds or till heated; transfer to a large plate. Combine cabbage, cucumber, avocado, quinoa, red onion, pepper, and feta cheese in a large mixing bowl.
- Inside a mixing bowl, combine the lemon juice, olive oil, sea salt, Dijon

mustard, and black pepper till the oil is emulsified; pour over the salad.

12. Zucchini and Chickpeas Salad

Preparation time: 10 minutes | **Cooking time:** 0 minutes | **Servings:** 3

Nutritional Value: Calories: 258 | Fat: 12g | Carbohydrates: 19g | Protein: 6g

Ingredients:

- 1/3 cup of chopped basil leaves
- 1 chopped garlic clove
- 1 pinch of red pepper flakes, crushed
- ½ cup of crumbled feta cheese
- 2 cups of diced zucchini
- ½ teaspoon of oregano
- 1 tablespoon of capers, drained & chopped
- ½ cup of chopped Kalamata olives
- 1 can of drained chickpeas
- ½ cup of chopped sweet onion
- 1/3 cup of olive oil
- ¾ cup of chopped red bell pepper
- 1 tablespoon of chopped rosemary
- ¼ cup of balsamic vinegar
- Salt & pepper, to taste

Instructions:

- Inside a large-sized mixing bowl, combine the vegetables and cover well.
- Allow to cool completely before serving. Refrigerate the bowl for a

few hours before serving to allow the flavors to meld.

13. Spinach and Feta Topped Pita

Preparation time: 5 minutes | **Cooking time:** 25 minutes | **Servings:** 6

Nutritional Value: Calories: 350 | Fat: 17g | Carbohydrates: 9g | Protein: 11g

Ingredients:

- 4 sliced mushrooms
- 2 chopped Roma - plum tomatoes
- 0.5 cups of crumbled feta cheese
- 1 bunch of spinach
- 6 oz. tub of sun-dried tomato pesto
- 6 6-inches whole-wheat pita bread
- 3 tablespoons of olive oil
- 2 tablespoons of grated Parmesan cheese
- Black pepper

Instructions:

- Preheat oven to 350°F.
- Place each pita on a baking sheet and brush with pesto on one side. (pesto-side up).
- Before cooking, rinse and chop the spinach. Spinach, feta cheese, mushrooms, tomatoes, pepper, pepper, Parmesan cheese, and a splash of oil are piled on top of the pitas.
- Crisp the pita bread in the oven. (for around 12 minutes). Pita bread should be cut into quarters.

14. Vegetable Couscous Curry

Preparation time: 10 minutes | **Cooking time:** 35 minutes | **Servings:** 4

Nutritional Value: Calories: 209 | Fat: 4g | Carbohydrates: 41g | Protein: 6g

Ingredients:

- 1 1/2 cups of vegetable stock
- 3 minced cloves of garlic
- 1 teaspoon of olive oil
- 1/4 cup of golden raisins
- 1 small leek, thinly sliced
- 1 grated carrot
- 1/2 chopped red bell pepper
- 1 pinch of ground turmeric
- 1/2 small chopped onion
- 1 teaspoon of curry powder
- 2 tablespoons of sliced almonds
- 1/2 cup of couscous
- 1 thinly sliced stalk of celery
- Salt and ground black pepper
- 2 tomatoes - seeded, peeled, and chopped
- 1/4 cup of dried currants

Instructions:

- Add the oil to a skillet over medium flame and sauté the onion, leek, red bell pepper, celery, and garlic till the onion is translucent about 5 minutes.

- After bringing the vegetable stock to a boil, add the carrots, tomatoes, couscous, raisins, and currants. Bring to a boil again and season with curry powder, salt, turmeric, and black pepper. Reduce the flame to low, cover, and leave to cook for 10 minutes.

- Remove the pan from the flame. Allow 5 minutes for the couscous to absorb the liquid.

15. Spinach Rice

Preparation time: 10 minutes | **Cooking time:** 30 minutes | **Servings:** 4

Nutritional Value: Calories 410 | Total fat 4.4g | Protein 8.3g | Carbs 82.5g

Ingredients:

- 1 large minced carrot
- 1 1/2 cups of fresh spinach
- 1 small minced onion
- 4 chopped green Chile peppers
- 1 teaspoon of garlic and ginger paste
- 1 tablespoon of olive oil, or as needed
- 1 teaspoon of coriander powder roasted
- 4 1/2 cups of water, or more as needed
- 1 pinch of salt, or to taste
- 1 teaspoon of cumin seeds
- 2 cups of white rice uncooked

Instructions:

- Warm the oil inside a skillet over medium flame and cook the cumin seeds, stirring constantly, for 1 minute or till fragrant. Cook for 5 minutes or until the carrot, onion, and green Chile peppers are tender. Cook for 2 minutes after adding the ginger-garlic powder.

- In a blender, combine spinach leaves until paste forms. Cook for 2 to 3 minutes, stirring constantly, or until all of the water from the spinach has evaporated.

- In a mixing bowl, combine spinach, rice, salt, and coriander powder. Fill halfway with water in a rice cooker, then add the rice mixture.

- Cook the spinach rice for about 15 minutes in a rice cooker, according to the manufacturer's instructions.

16. Zucchini Soup

Preparation time: 10 minutes | **Cooking time:** 25 minutes | **Servings:** 4

Nutritional Value: Calories: 172 | Fat: 15g | Carbohydrates: 9g | Protein: 4g

Ingredients:

- 2 1/2 cups of chicken broth
- Sour cream and fresh dill for garnish
- 1 1/2 pounds of zucchini
- Salt & black pepper to taste
- 2 cloves of minced garlic
- 1 tablespoon of olive oil
- 1/2 cup of heavy cream
- 1 small diced onion

Instructions:

- Zucchini should be peeled and diced into 1/2" cubes.

- Cook garlic and onion in olive oil till softened over medium flame. Cook for another 5 minutes or till the zucchini is tender.

- Season to taste using salt, broth, and pepper. Cook, covered, for 10-15 minutes, till the zucchini is soft.

- Puree the broth using a hand blender. Cook for another minute after adding the cream.

- Season to taste using salt and pepper. Serve topped with a dollop of sour cream and a sprig of fresh dill.

17. Creamy Asparagus Soup

Preparation time: 10 minutes | **Cooking time:** 30 minutes | **Servings:** 4

Nutritional Value: Calories: 181 | Fat: 14g | Carbohydrates: 11g | Protein: 5g

Ingredients:

- 1 clove of minced garlic

- 1/2 teaspoon of fresh lemon juice

- 1 diced small onion

- 2 1/4 cups of chicken broth

- 1 tablespoon of butter

- For serving parmesan cheese

- 1/2 cup of heavy cream

- 1 1/2 pounds of trimmed and washed asparagus

- Salt and black pepper, to taste

Instructions:

- Asparagus should be cut in half to make "slices."

- Cook garlic and onion in oil until soft over a moderate flame. Cook for 5 minutes more after adding the asparagus.

- To taste, season with salt, broth, and pepper. Cook for 15-20 minutes or until the asparagus is tender.

- Using a hand blender, puree the soup until completely smooth. Mix in the cream and fresh lemon juice.

- Season with more salt and black pepper if desired.

18. Mediterranean Stew

Preparation time: 10 minutes | **Cooking time:** 10 hours | **Servings:** 10

Nutritional Value: Calories: 122 | Fat: 2g | Carbohydrates: 30g | Protein: 4g

Ingredients:

- ⅓ cup of raisins

- 1 chopped tomato

- ½ teaspoon of ground cumin

- 1 cubed squash butternut

- ½ cup of vegetable broth

- 2 cups of cubed eggplant,

- ¼ teaspoon of paprika

- 2 cups of cubed zucchini

- 1 cup of tomato sauce

- ¼ teaspoon of ground cinnamon

- 1 clove of chopped garlic

- ¼ teaspoon of crushed red pepper

- 1 sliced carrot

- 10 oz. of okra

- 1 cup chopped onion
- ½ teaspoon of ground turmeric

Instructions:

- Combine butternut squash and eggplant in a slow cooker, then add zucchini, okra, broth, peas, carrots, tomato sauce, cabbage, raisins, and garlic. Seasonings include cumin seed, turmeric, red pepper, and cinnamon.
- Cover and cook on low for 9 to 10 hours or until the vegetables are softened.

19. Herbed Quinoa and Cauliflower Casserole

Preparation time: 10 minutes | Cooking time: 25 minutes | Servings: 5

Nutritional Value: Calories 239 | Total fat 12.2g | Protein 16g | Carbs 16.1g

Ingredients:

- 2/3 cup of cooked quinoa
- 4 cups of cauliflower florets (480 g)
- 1 cup of low-fat milk
- 2 tablespoons of butter
- 4 oz. of grated skim-part mozzarella cheese
- 2/3 cup of cottage cheese crumbled
- 1/4 cup of parsley
- 4 oz. of grated mozzarella cheese

- Sea salt and freshly ground black pepper

Instructions:

- Preheat oven to 360°F.
- In a saucepan, bring to a boil. After adding the cauliflower florets, cook for 1 minute. Set aside after draining.
- In a mixing bowl, combine cauliflower florets, parsley, low-fat milk, butter, cooked quinoa, and crumbled cottage cheese. Season with salt and pepper to taste. Combine everything thoroughly.
- Fill a casserole dish halfway with the mixture. Top with mozzarella cheese.
- Bake for 20–25 minutes or until the cheese is completely melted.

20. Bean Sprout Salad

Cooking time:

30 minutes

Servings

4

Nutritional Value:

Calories 121

Total fat 8g

Protein 4g

Carbs 9g

Ingredients:

- 2 tablespoons of peanuts crushed for garnish

- 3 cups of washed and drained bean sprouts

- 1 julienned or shredded carrot

- 2 tablespoons of chopped cilantro, and extra for the garnish

- 1 finely sliced green onion

- 2 cups of grated green cabbage

For the Dressing:

- 1 tablespoon of soy sauce

- 1/4 teaspoon of grated fresh ginger

- 1 tablespoon of honey

- 1/2 teaspoon of sesame oil

- 1 1/2 tablespoons of rice vinegar

- 1 tablespoon of olive oil

Instructions:

- Inside a small-sized cup, whisk together the dressing ingredients.

- Inside a large-sized mixing bowl, combine the cabbage, bean sprouts, carrots, and cilantro.

- Toss in the dressing to combine. Refrigerate for one hour, stirring every now and then.

- Before serving, garnish with chopped green onion and crushed peanuts.

Chapter 7: Fish and Shellfish

1. Tuna with Olive and Kale

Preparation time: 10 minutes | **Cooking time:** 15 minutes | **Servings:** 6

Nutritional Value: Calories: 242 | Fat: 11g | Carbohydrates: 24g | Protein: 7g

Ingredients:

- ¼ teaspoon of kosher salt
- 2 (6-ounces) cans of tuna in olive oil, un-drained
- ¼ cup of capers
- 3 tablespoons of olive oil
- 2 teaspoons of honey
- ¼ teaspoon of black pepper
- 1 (2.25-ounces) can of sliced olives, drained
- 1 cup of chopped onion
- 3 minced garlic cloves
- ¼ teaspoon of crushed red pepper
- 1-pound of chopped kale
- 1 (15-ounces) can of cannellini beans

Instructions:

- Soak the kale in boiling water for about 2 minutes, then drain and set aside. Heat the oil in a medium-large cooking pot over a moderate flame. Stir in the onion until it is translucent and soft. Cook for 1 minute or until the garlic is fragrant.
- Stir in the capers, olives, and red pepper for about 1 minute. Kale that has been cooked and honey should be combined. Cook for 8-10 minutes, covered, over a low flame, stirring occasionally. Mix in the tuna, beans, pepper, and salt. Serve hot after thoroughly stirring.

2. Fish and Lentil Patties

Preparation time: 10 minutes | **Cooking time:** 25 minutes | **Servings:** 4

Nutritional Value: Calories 276 | Total Fat 10.1g | Protein 22.7g | Carbs 23.4g

Ingredients:

- 1 cup of cooked lentils
- 2/3 cup of breadcrumbs
- 1 whole whisked egg
- 1 medium red bell pepper deseeded and chopped
- 2 tablespoons of olive oil

- 1 celery stalk chopped

- 10 oz. of flaked and steamed cream dory fillets

- 1/2 cup of chopped onion

- 1 teaspoon of dried thyme

- 2 tablespoons of chopped cilantro

- 1/2 teaspoon of garlic powder

- Kosher salt and freshly ground black pepper

Instructions:

- On a serving platter, flake cooked dory fillets with a fork.

- Inside a large-sized mixing bowl, combine all of the ingredients, season with pepper and salt, and thoroughly mix.

- 1/4 cup of the mixture should be used to make each patty.

- Warm the olive oil in a large nonstick skillet before adding the patties.

- Cook for 10 to 15 minutes, stirring occasionally, or until golden brown.

3. Herbs and Cheese Salmon Frittata

Preparation time: 10 minutes | **Cooking time:** 25 minutes | **Servings:** 5

Nutritional Value: Calories 217 | Total Fat 12.5g | Protein 18.8g | Carbs 4.7g

Ingredients:

- 2 oz. of skim-part grated cheddar

- 1 clove of garlic minced

- 2 tablespoons of fresh dill weed chopped

- 6 whole eggs

- 2 tablespoons of olive oil

- 1 chopped medium white onion

- 8 oz. of salmon diced and baked

- 2 tablespoons of fresh parsley chopped

- Kosher salt and freshly ground black pepper

Instructions:

- Preheat the oven to 380°F.

- Combine 6 eggs, pepper, and salt inside a large-sized mixing bowl.

- For about 3 minutes, stir fry onion and garlic in warm oil in a medium-sized skillet over medium flame. Cook for another 2-3 minutes, stirring in the salmon and dill.

- Fill a baking dish halfway with the mixture. Pour the beaten egg mixture over the top, followed by the cheddar cheese.

- Bake at 350°F for about 15 minutes.

- Garnish with chopped parsley just before serving.

4. Salmon, Carrot, and Zucchini Patties

Preparation time: 10 minutes | **Cooking time:** 25 minutes | **Servings:** 8

Nutritional Value: Calories 192 | Total Fat 10g | Protein 14g | Carbs 11g

Ingredients:

- 1 grated zucchini medium

- Salt and pepper, to taste

- 2 whole eggs beaten

- 1/4 cup of all-purpose flour

- 2 tablespoons of olive oil

- 3/4 cup of breadcrumbs

- 2 tablespoons of chopped cilantro

- 16 oz. of canned flaked pink salmon drained and flaked

- 1 carrot grated

- 1/2 cup of fresh chives chopped

Instructions:

- Combine the salmon, eggs, zucchini, cilantro, breadcrumbs, almond flour, carrots, and chives inside a large-sized mixing bowl. Mix well after finishing with a sprinkling of pepper and salt.

- Warm 2 tablespoons olive oil in a nonstick pan, then form 1/2 cup of the mixture into patties and place in the pan. Repeat with the remaining mixture.

- Cook, stirring occasionally, for 15 minutes or until the top is lightly browned. Halfway through cooking, flip the patties.

5. Southwestern Catfish with Salsa

Preparation time: 10 minutes | **Cooking time:** 22 minutes | **Servings:** 4

Nutritional Value: Calories 107 | Total Fat 4g | Protein 9g | Carbs 10g

Ingredients:

- 2 finely chopped jalapeno peppers, remove the seeds

- 4 catfish fillets (6 ounces each)

- 1/4 cup of onion finely chopped

- 3 teaspoons of chili powder

- 1/2 teaspoon of garlic powder

- 3 teaspoons of paprika

- 2 tablespoons of white wine vinegar

- 1-1/2 teaspoons of ground cumin

- 2 tablespoons of olive oil extra-virgin

- 1 to 1-1/2 teaspoons of ground coriander

- 3 teaspoons of salt divided

- 1 teaspoon of cayenne pepper

- 3 chopped medium tomatoes

Instructions:

- Inside a large-sized mixing bowl, combine the jalapenos, vinegar, onion, tomatoes, and 1 teaspoon salt to make the salsa. After wrapping, place in the refrigerator for at least 30 minutes.

- Sprinkle the catfish with paprika, chili powder, cumin, cayenne pepper, remaining salt, coriander, and garlic powder.

- Heat 2 tablespoons of olive oil in a nonstick skillet over medium flame.

- Cook for 12 to 15 minutes, or until the fish flakes easily with a fork; flip the fish gently halfway through cooking. Serve with salsa on the side.

6. Tomato-Basil Fish

Preparation time: 10 minutes | **Cooking time:** 15 minutes | **Servings:** 2

Nutritional Value: Calories 121 | Total Fat 4g | Protein 18g | Carbs 4g

Ingredients:

- 1/8 teaspoon of pepper

- 2 teaspoons of Parmesan cheese grated

- 1/4 teaspoon of dried basil

- 2 plum tomatoes thinly sliced

- 1 tablespoon of lemon juice

- 8 ounces of haddock fillets, red snapper, or cod

- 1/8 teaspoon of salt

- 1 teaspoon of olive oil extra-virgin

Instructions:

- Warm a large skillet over a moderate flame.

- Inside a shallow bowl, combine the lemon juice and oil. Combine the fish fillets with the mixture. Season with salt and pepper to taste, and sprinkle half of the basil over the fish fillet. Top with the tomatoes, then the cheese, and the remaining seasonings.

- Cook for 12 to 15 minutes or till the fish easily flakes with a fork.

7. Salmon with Fennel Salad

Preparation time: 10 minutes | **Cooking time:** 25 minutes | **Servings:** 4

Nutritional Value: Calories 464 | Total Fat 30g | Protein 38g | Carbs 9g

Ingredients:

- 1 teaspoon of finely chopped fresh thyme

- 2 tablespoons of chopped fresh dill

- 4 skinless center-cut salmon fillets

- 2 tablespoons of orange juice fresh (1 orange)

- 1 teaspoon of fresh lemon juice

- 2/3 cup of 2% reduced-fat Greek yogurt

- 1 clove of garlic grated

- 2 teaspoons of finely chopped fresh flat-leaf parsley

- 1 teaspoon of kosher salt divided

- 2 tablespoons of olive oil extra-virgin

- 4 cups of thinly sliced fennel (from 2 [15-oz.] heads of fennel)

Instructions:

- Combine the parsley, thyme, and 1/2 teaspoon of salt in a shallow mixing bowl. After brushing the salmon using oil, lightly sprinkle the herb mixture on top.

- Heat 2 tablespoons of olive oil inside a nonstick skillet and add salmon fillets. Cook for a total of 10 to 12 minutes.

- In a medium-sized mixing bowl, combine the fennel, garlic, lemon juice, yogurt, orange juice, dill, and the remaining 1/2 teaspoon salt. Serve the salmon fillets with a side of fennel salad.

8. Cod Mushroom Stew

Preparation time: 10 minutes | **Cooking time:** 20 minutes | **Servings:** 6

Nutritional Value: Calories: 238 | Fat: 7g | Carbohydrates: 15g | Protein: 4g

Ingredients:

- ¼ teaspoon of black pepper
- 2 cups of chopped onion
- 1 ½ pounds of cod fillets, cut into 1-inch pieces

- 2 minced garlic cloves

- ¾ teaspoon of smoked paprika

- 1 (12-ounces) jar of roasted red peppers

- 2 tablespoons of olive oil

- 1 cup of black olives

- 1/3 cup of dry red wine

- 3 cups of sliced mushrooms

- 1 can of tomato

- ¼ teaspoon of kosher salt

Instructions:

- Warm the oil inside a medium-sized frying pan over a medium flame. After adding the onions, cook for another 4 minutes. Cook for 1 minute, stirring frequently, after adding the garlic and smoked paprika. Toss roasted peppers, tomatoes, wine vinegar, juice, pepper, olives, and salt together gently. Bring to a boil. Reduce the flame to medium-low and add the cod and mushrooms. Cook until the fish is flaky, stirring occasionally. Serve immediately and enjoy.

9. Fish Soup

Preparation time: 10 minutes | **Cooking time:** 30 minutes | **Servings:** 6

Nutritional Value: Calories 222 | Total fat 3g | Protein 31.3g | Carbs 11.9g

Ingredients:

- 2 1/2 ounces of canned mushrooms
- 1/2 cup of dry white wine
- 1 chopped onion

- 1/4 cup of black olives sliced
- 2 cans of chicken broth (14 ounces)
- 1 teaspoon of dried basil
- 2 cloves of minced garlic
- 1/2 chopped green bell pepper
- 1 can of diced tomatoes (14.5 ounces)
- 1/8 teaspoon of ground black pepper
- 1 pound of peeled and deveined medium shrimp
- 2 bay leaves
- 1/2 cup of orange juice
- 1 can of tomato sauce (8 ounces)
- 1/4 teaspoon of crushed fennel seed
- 1 pound of cubed cod fillets

Instructions:

- Inside a cooker, combine the onion, tomatoes, dried basil, green bell pepper, garlic, bay leaves, chicken broth, mushrooms, tomato sauce, olives, orange juice, wine, fennel seeds, and pepper. Cook for 20 minutes or until the vegetables are tender.

- Mix in the shrimp and cod. After covering, cook for 10 minutes or until the shrimp is completely opaque. Bay leaves should be removed and discarded.

10. Sicilian Fish Stew

Preparation time: 10 minutes | **Cooking time:** 35 minutes | **Servings:** 6

Nutritional Value: Calories: 320 | Fat: 12g | Carbohydrates: 20g | Protein: 31g

Ingredients:

- ¾ cup of dry white wine
- Salt to taste
- 1 chopped yellow onion
- Olive oil
- 3 1/2 cups of plum tomatoes
- Black pepper to taste
- 2 lbs. of sliced skinless sea bass fillet
- ¼ cup of golden raisins
- Italian bread for the serving
- 2 tablespoons of capers
- ½ teaspoon of dried thyme
- 1 tablespoon of toasted pine nuts
- A pinch of red pepper flakes
- ½ cup of chopped parsley leaves
- 2 chopped celery ribs
- Tomato juice
- 3 cups of vegetable broth
- 4 minced garlic cloves

Instructions:

- In a Dutch oven, cook onions and celery with black pepper and salt for about 4 minutes on medium flame, stirring constantly.

- Cook for 1 minute after adding the thyme, flakes, and garlic.

- Allow the tomato juice and white wine to simmer together.

- Add the capers, raisins, tomatoes, and stock when the liquid has been reduced to half its original volume.

- Cook for another 20 minutes.

- Before adding the fish to the cooking liquid, season it with salt and black pepper. Allow 5 minutes to bring to a gentle simmer.

- Remove the pan from the flame and set it aside to cool for 5 minutes.

- If desired, garnish with parsley and pine nuts.

11. Mediterranean Salmon

Preparation time: 10 minutes | **Cooking time:** 20 minutes | **Servings:** 2

Nutritional Value: Calories: 322 | Fat: 10g | Carbohydrates: 15g | Protein: 31g

Ingredients:

- 1/8 teaspoon of black pepper

- 1 tablespoon of capers

- 1/2 tablespoon of olive oil

- 2 salmon fillets, skinless & 6 ounces each

- 1/4 cup of zucchini, chopped finely

- 1 cup of cherry tomatoes

- 1.25 ounces of ripe olives, sliced

- 1/8 teaspoon of sea salt

Instructions:

- Preheat the oven to 400°F and season the fish on both sides with salt and black pepper. After spraying the baking dish with cooking spray, arrange the fish in a single layer.

- Combine the tomatoes and remaining ingredients in a mixing bowl, spoon the mixture over the fillets, and bake for about 22 minutes. Enjoy while it is still warm.

12. Tilapia with Avocado and Red Onion

Preparation time: 10 minutes | **Cooking time:** 10 minutes | **Servings:** 4

Nutritional Value: Calories: 200 | Fat: 3g | Carbohydrates: 4g | Protein: 22g

Ingredients:

- 1 tablespoon of freshly squeezed orange juice

- ¼ cup of chopped red onion

- 4 (4 ounces) of tilapia fillets, skinned

- 1 tablespoon of olive oil

- ¼ teaspoon of kosher salt

- 1 avocado

Instructions:

- Combine the oil, orange juice, and salt in a 9-inch glass pie plate. Place the fillets in the pie dish and coat all sides while working on them simultaneously. Make a wagon wheel out of the fillets.

- Add 1 tablespoon of onion in the center of each fillet; fold in half over the onion at the end of the fillet that hangs over the edge. When you're done, you should have four folded-over fillets against the dish's outer edge, with the ends all in the center.

- Cover the dish with plastic wrap, leaving a small gap at the top for steam to escape. In the microwave, cook for 3 minutes on high. When lightly pressed with a fork, it should split into flakes. (chunks). Serve the fillets with avocado as a garnish.

13. Salmon with Asparagus

Preparation time: 10 minutes | **Cooking time:** 22 minutes | **Servings:** 4

Nutritional Value: Calories 491 | Total Fat 34g | Protein 37g | Carbs 11g

Ingredients:

- 1/2 cup of melted butter
- 1 teaspoon of black pepper
- 1 teaspoon of paprika
- 2 teaspoons of fresh basil
- 1 pound of asparagus, trim the spear ends
- 4 fillets of salmon
- Fresh basil for garnishing
- 1 lemon juiced
- 1 tablespoon of minced garlic
- Lemon wedges for garnishing
- 1 teaspoon of salt
- 1 lemon sliced
- 1 teaspoon of garlic powder

Instructions:

- Cut four heavy-duty foil sheets 12 x 18 inches in half. Place two lemon slices on each sheet of foil. Garlic powder, paprika, salt, and pepper are rubbed into the salmon. Each salmon fillet will be centered in the lemon slices. Place the asparagus in four equal portions on each foil piece next to the salmon.
- Inside a small-sized cup, combine the fresh lemon juice, garlic, melted butter, and fresh basil. Evenly distribute the butter mixture over the salmon and asparagus.
- Wrap the salmon and asparagus in foil, sealing the edges to create a packet.
- Lay the foil packages out on a baking sheet. Bake for around 12 to 15 minutes at 400°F. Sprinkle the salmon with basil and lemon juice before serving.

14. Greek Fish

Preparation time: 10 minutes | **Cooking time:** 25 minutes | **Servings:** 4

Nutritional Value: Calories 246 | Total Fat 12g | Protein 29g | Carbs 6g

Ingredients:

- 1/2 red onion, small, thinly sliced
- 1/4 teaspoon of salt
- 2 tablespoons of olive oil
- 1/4 cup of Greek olives sliced and pitted
- 4 COD fillets (6 ounces each)
- 1 can of tomato sauce (8 ounces)
- 1/4 cup of crumbled feta cheese
- 1 green pepper small, make thin strips

- 1/8 teaspoon of pepper

Instructions:

- In an oiled baking dish, spread the cod. Drizzle with extra virgin olive oil and season with salt and pepper. Spread tomato sauce and cheese on top of the olives, green pepper, and onion.

- Bake at 390°F for 12 to 15 minutes or until the fish flakes easily with a fork.

15. Mediterranean Tilapia

Preparation time: 10 minutes | **Cooking time:** 15 minutes | **Servings:** 6

Nutritional Value: Calories 197 | Total Fat 4g | Protein 34g | Carbs 5g

Ingredients:

- 1/2 cup of artichoke hearts water-packed chopped

- 6 tilapia fillets (6 ounces each)

- 1/2 cup of sliced ripe olives

- 1 cup of canned Italian tomatoes diced

- 1/2 cup of crumbled feta cheese

Instructions:

- Preheat the oven to 390 degrees Fahrenheit.

- Place the fillets on a lightly greased baking sheet. Top with artichoke hearts, tomatoes, cheese, and olives.

- Bake for 10 to 12 minutes or until the fish is flaky.

Chapter 8: Meat Recipes

1. Sautéed Chicken with Olives, Capers, and Lemons

Preparation time: 5 minutes | **Cooking time:** 30 minutes | **Servings:** 4

Nutritional Value: Calories: 595 | Fat: 34g | Carbohydrates: 6g | Protein: 51g

Ingredients:

- 6 boneless chicken thighs
- 2 tablespoons of all-purpose flour
- 1 minced garlic clove minced
- 2 tablespoons of parsley
- 1/4 cup of capers
- 2 sliced lemons
- 1 cup of chicken broth
- 3/4 cup of Sicilian green olives
- Black pepper to taste
- 2/4 cup of olive oil
- Kosher salt to taste
- 2 tablespoons of butter

Instructions:

- Toss the salt, chicken, and pepper together inside a mixing bowl. Allow 15 minutes for this to take place.
- Cook half of the lemon slices in hot olive oil for about five minutes on both sides over medium flame.
- Arrange the cooked browned lemon slices in a circle on the platter.
- Coat the chicken in rice flour and cook it for seven minutes on both sides inside a skillet with hot olive oil. Place the cooked chicken on a platter and serve.
- In the same pan, heat the oil and sauté the garlic for 30 seconds. Combine the olives, chicken broth, lemons, and capers. Cook for a few minutes on high flame.
- When half of the liquid has been absorbed, stir in the parsley and butter. Allow one minute for cooking.
- Season to taste using salt and pepper.

2. Chicken with Tomato-Balsamic Pan Sauce

Preparation time: 10 minutes | **Cooking time:** 25 minutes | **Servings:** 4

Nutritional Value: Calories: 294 | Fat: 17g | Carbohydrates: 10g | Protein: 2g

Ingredients:

- 1 tablespoon of minced garlic
- ¼ cup of balsamic vinegar
- 3 tablespoons of olive oil
- ½ teaspoon of ground pepper
- 1 tablespoon of toasted fennel seeds, crushed
- ½ teaspoon of salt
- 2 (8 oz.) of boneless chicken breasts, skinless
- 1 tablespoon of butter
- ½ cup of halved cherry tomatoes
- 2 tablespoons of sliced shallot

Instructions:

- Using a mallet, pound the chicken breasts into four pieces to a thickness of 1/4 inch. Heat 2 tablespoons of oil inside a skillet over a medium-high flame and season the chicken using 1/4 teaspoon of pepper and salt. Cook for 3 minutes on each side of the chicken breasts. Cover with foil and place on a serving plate to keep warm.

- In a pan, combine one tablespoon of oil, the shallot, and the tomatoes and cook until softened. Bring the mixture to a boil, then reduce the vinegar in half. Cook, stirring occasionally, for four minutes with the fennel seeds, salt, garlic, and pepper. Remove from the flame and add the butter. Serve the chicken with this sauce.

3. Chicken Stuffed with Asparagus

Preparation time: 10 minutes | **Cooking time:** 30 minutes | **Servings:** 2

Nutritional Value: Calories 390 | Total Fat 10.8g | Protein 57.4g | Carbs 13.3g

Ingredients:

- 1/4 cup of Italian seasoned bread crumbs
- 8 asparagus spears trimmed, divided
- Salt and black pepper to taste
- 2 large halves of chicken breast boneless and skinless
- 1/2 cup of skim-part grated mozzarella cheese, divided

Instructions:

- Preheat the oven to 400 degrees Fahrenheit.

- Place each chicken breast on a solid, level surface between two heavy plastic sheets. Pound the chicken to an even thickness of 1/4 inch with the smooth side of a meat mallet. Season both sides liberally with salt and pepper.

- In the center of each chicken breast, place four asparagus spears and 1/4 cup of mozzarella cheese. To make a neat, compact roll, wrap the remaining chicken breasts around the asparagus and cheese. Place on a sprayed baking sheet and sprinkle with crumbs.

- Bake for approximately 20 to 25 minutes.

4. Greek Chicken

Preparation time: 20 minutes | **Cooking time:** 3 hours | **Servings:** 4

Nutritional Value: Calories: 399 | Fat: 17g | Carbohydrates: 12g | Protein: 50g

Ingredients:

- 3 tablespoons of red wine vinegar
- 1 cup of Kalamata olives
- 1 tablespoon of olive oil
- ¼ teaspoon of black pepper
- 1 teaspoon of honey
- ½ cup of feta cheese
- 1 teaspoon of dried thyme
- 2 pounds of boneless chicken breasts
- 1 medium red onion chunks
- ½ teaspoon of kosher salt
- 1 teaspoon of dried oregano
- Chopped fresh herbs: a combination of parsley, basil, or thyme (optional for the serving)
- 1 tablespoon of minced garlic
- 1 (12-ounces) jar of roasted red peppers

Instructions:

- Apply olive oil to the slow cooker. Inside a large-sized skillet over medium flame, heat the olive oil. Season the chicken breasts on both sides. In the hot oil, sear the chicken breasts on all sides. (around 3 minutes).

- When it's done, transfer it to the slow cooker. Combine the chicken breasts, red peppers, olives, and red onion. Arrange veggies around the chicken instead of directly on top of it.

- Combine the garlic, oregano, vinegar, honey, and thyme in a small-sized mixing bowl. Pour it over the chicken once everything has been combined. Cook for about 3 hours on low or until the chicken is no longer pinkish in the center. Serve

with fresh herbs and crumbled feta cheese.

5. Chicken and Orzo Soup

Preparation time: 10 minutes | **Cooking time:** 30 minutes | **Servings:** 4

Nutritional Value: Calories: 248 | Fat: 4g | Carbohydrates: 23g | Protein: 25g

Ingredients:

- 12 ounces of skinless and boneless chicken breasts
- 1 tablespoon of olive oil
- ½ cup of sliced carrot
- ½ cup of chopped celery
- Salt & ground pepper to taste
- ½ cup of orzo
- 6 cups of low-sodium and fat-free chicken broth

- ½ cup of chopped white onion
- Lemon halves to squeeze
- ¼ cup of chopped fresh dill

Instructions:

- Inside a large-sized pot, heat the olive oil over a medium flame. Cook until the onion and celery are soft, stirring occasionally. Toss in the chicken broth, carrots, and chicken, and season to taste with pepper and salt. Bring to a boil, then reduce to a low flame and cook for 20 minutes or until the chicken is thoroughly cooked. Remove the chicken from the soup and cool before shredding it into bite-sized pieces. While shredding the chicken, keep the broth pot covered and on medium flame. Return the stock to boil, then add the orzo and cook for 8 minutes. Remove the saucepan from the flame, add the chicken and dill to the broth, and season with a squeeze of lemon juice before serving.

6. Chicken and Vegetable Soup

Preparation time: 10 minutes | **Cooking time:** 35 minutes | **Servings:** 4

Nutritional Value: Calories: 272 | Fat: 9g | Carbohydrates: 22g | Protein: 27g

Ingredients:

- 2 peeled potatoes and make 1/2" cubes
- 1 diced onion
- 14 1/2 ounces can of diced tomatoes with the juices
- 4 cups of chicken broth
- 2 tablespoons of butter

- 2 cups of cooked chicken
- 1/2 teaspoon of dried oregano
- 2 cups of frozen mixed vegetables
- 1 tablespoon of flour
- 2 teaspoons of chopped fresh parsley
- 1/2 teaspoon of dried basil

Instructions:

- Cook the onion in the oil for 3 minutes on medium flame or until softened.
- After adding the potatoes, cook for 3-4 minutes. After adding the flour, cook for another minute.
- Combine the broth, tomatoes, and seasonings. Cook for about 15 minutes, stirring occasionally, or until the potatoes are tender.
- Combine the vegetables and chicken. Cook for an additional 10 minutes.
- Season to taste with salt and pepper.
- Before serving, garnish with parsley.

7. Chicken with Onions, Figs, Potatoes, and Carrots

Preparation time: 10 minutes | **Cooking time:** 45 minutes | **Servings:** 4

Nutritional Value: Calories: 429 | Fat: 4g | Carbohydrates: 27g | Protein: 52g

Ingredients:

- 2 tablespoons of chopped fresh parsley leaves
- 4 chicken leg-thigh quarters
- 1 teaspoon of sea salt divided

- 2 cups of fingerling potatoes, halved
- 4 fresh figs, quartered
- 2 tablespoons of olive oil
- ¼ teaspoon of ground black pepper
- 2 julienned carrots

Instructions:

- Preheat the oven to 425 degrees Fahrenheit. Toss the potatoes, figs, and carrots in a small bowl with olive oil, 1/2 teaspoon of sea salt, and pepper. Fill a 9-by-13-inch baking dish halfway with the mixture.

- Add the remaining teaspoon of salt to the chicken. It should be placed alongside the vegetables. Bake until the vegetables are tender and the chicken is 165°F on the inside. If desired, garnish with parsley.

8. Chicken with Basil-Lemon Gravy

Preparation time: 10 minutes | **Cooking time:** 30 minutes | **Servings:** 4

Nutritional Value: Calories 193 | Total Fat 8.4g | Protein 23.8g | Carbs 4.6g

Ingredients:

- 3 tablespoons of chopped fresh basil
- 4 chicken breast halves boned and skinned
- 1 tablespoon of lemon zest
- 2 tablespoons of almond flour
- 1 cup of chicken stock
- 3 tablespoons of fresh lemon juice

- 2 tablespoons of butter

Instructions:

- Place the chicken breasts on a cutting board. Flatten slightly with the smooth side of a meat mallet. On all sides, coat the chicken with flour. Melt the butter inside a large-sized skillet over a medium-high flame. Cook chicken breasts in a skillet until lightly browned on both sides, about 6 minutes per side. Take the fillets out of the pan.

- Meanwhile, in the same pan, combine the fresh lemon juice, chicken stock, basil, and lemon zest. Cook for 5 minutes with the lid on. Cook for another 5 minutes after adding the cooked chicken.

- Cook for another 5 minutes or until the sauce thickens. Place the chicken on a platter to serve. Put the sauce over the chicken and serve.

9. Chicken Shawarma Pitas

Preparation time: 10 minutes | **Cooking time:** 30 minutes | **Servings:** 6

Nutritional Value: Calories: 320 | Fat: 15g | Carbohydrates: 4g | Protein: 40g

Ingredients:

- ¾ tablespoon of garlic powder
- ¾ tablespoon of coriander
- 1 tablespoon of lemon juice
- ½ teaspoon of cloves
- 8 boneless chicken
- ¾ tablespoon of cumin
- 1/3 cup of olive oil
- 1 sliced onion

- ½ teaspoon of cayenne pepper
- Tahini sauce
- ¾ tablespoon of paprika
- Pita bread
- ¾ tablespoon of turmeric powder
- Salt to taste

Instructions:

- Combine the sliced chicken, onions, salt, paprika, turmeric, cumin, garlic, cloves, lemon juice, olive oil, and coriander in a mixing bowl. To coat the chicken evenly, toss well. Refrigerate for at least 3 hours.
- Place the chicken pieces and marinade in an oil-coated baking dish.
- Preheat oven to 425°F and bake for 30 minutes.
- Top pita bread with tahini sauce and roasted chicken pieces. Include your favorite salad as well.
- Serve right away and enjoy.

10. Sheet Pan Chicken and Veggies

Preparation time: 10 minutes | **Cooking time:** 45 minutes | **Servings:** 6

Nutritional Value: Calories: 357 | Fat: 14g | Carbohydrates: 28g | Protein: 28g

Ingredients:

- 6 cups of baby spinach
- 2 lbs. of russet potatoes
- 6 chicken thighs
- 1 chopped onion

- 1 teaspoon of powdered rosemary
- 1/2 teaspoon of paprika
- 3/4 teaspoon of pepper
- 3 minced garlic cloves
- 1.25 teaspoons of salt
- 2 tablespoons of olive oil

Instructions:

- In a mixing bowl, combine the onion, rosemary, oil, garlic, potatoes, salt, and pepper.
- Place the potato mixture on a baking sheet sprayed with cooking spray.
- In a separate bowl, combine the salt, paprika, pepper, and rosemary; sprinkle over the chicken.
- At 400°F, bake the chicken pieces on top of the potato mixture for about 35 minutes.
- Remove the chicken from the oven and transfer it to a serving dish.
- After adding the spinach, bake for another 10 minutes.
- Serve the chicken with the cooked vegetables on the side.

11. Chicken Breasts Stuffed with Spinach and Feta

Preparation time: 10 minutes | **Cooking time:** 45 minutes | **Servings:** 4

Nutritional Value: Calories: 263 | Fat: 3g | Carbohydrates: 7g | Protein: 17g

Ingredients:

- 1-pound of fresh baby spinach
- ½ teaspoon of sea salt

- Zest of 1 lemon
- 2 tablespoons of olive oil
- 1/8 teaspoon of ground black pepper
- 3 minced garlic cloves
- 4 boneless and skinless chicken breasts
- ½ cup of crumbled feta cheese

Instructions:

- Preheat oven to 350°F. Heat the olive oil until it shimmers over a medium flame. Mix in the spinach thoroughly. Cook, stirring constantly, until the spinach has wilted.

- Add the garlic, lemon zest, sea salt, and pepper. Cook, stirring constantly, for about 30 seconds. Allow the cheese to cool slightly before adding it to the recipe.

- Roll the chicken breasts around the filling after evenly coating them with the spinach and cheese mixture. Use toothpicks or butcher's twine to close the bag. Bake for 30 to 40 minutes in a 9-by-13-inch baking dish or until the chicken reaches an internal temperature of 165°F. Allow to cool for 5 minutes before slicing and serving.

12. Rosemary Turkey Patties

Preparation time: 10 minutes | **Cooking time:** 25 minutes | **Servings:** 6

Nutritional Value: Calories 203 | Total Fat 5.5g | Protein 25.2g | Carbs 11.9g

Ingredients:

- 1 tablespoon of Worcestershire sauce
- 1/2 teaspoon of Kosher salt
- 1 1/2 lbs. of lean ground turkey
- 1/4 teaspoon of ground black pepper
- 2 tablespoons of fresh rosemary chopped
- 1/2 cup of breadcrumbs
- 2 tablespoons of all-purpose flour
- 1/2 teaspoon of ground coriander
- 1 whole egg
- 1 teaspoon of garlic powder
- 2 tablespoons of olive oil extra-virgin
- 1 medium onion chopped

Instructions:

- Inside a large-sized mixing bowl, combine the ground turkey, onion, coriander, bread crumbs, cinnamon, egg, all-purpose flour, salt, Worcestershire sauce, garlic powder, and pepper. Mix the ingredients thoroughly with your fingertips.

- Form the turkey mixture into 8 patties. Make an indent with your thumb in the center of each patty to keep them from bunching up in the center.

- Cook the patties in a nonstick pan with two tablespoons of olive oil for 15 to 18 minutes.

13. Zesty Apricot Turkey

Preparation time: 10 minutes | **Cooking time:** 30 minutes | **Servings:** 4

Nutritional Value: Calories 200 | Total Fat 2g | Protein 27g | Carbs 18g

Ingredients:

- 1 tablespoon of wine vinegar white
- 1/8 teaspoon of hot pepper sauce
- 1/2 teaspoon of lemon zest grated
- 1 garlic clove minced
- 1/2 teaspoon of salt
- 2 breasts of turkey tenderloins (8 ounces each)
- 1/4 teaspoon of pepper
- 2 tablespoons of olive oil extra-virgin
- 1/3 cup of apricot spreadable fruit
- 1 tablespoon of honey

Instructions:

- In a microwave-safe bowl, melt the spreadable fruit, then add the vinegar, lemon zest, honey, garlic, and pepper sauce. Reserve 1/4 cup of the sauce for garnish. Season the turkey liberally with salt and pepper.
- Heat two tablespoons of olive oil in a nonstick skillet and add the turkey.
- Cook for about 20 minutes, brushing every minute or so with the remaining sauce. Allow for a 5-minute rest before slicing. Serve with the sauce you set aside earlier.

14. Chicken Tomato, Bean, and Pepper Roast

Preparation time: 10 minutes | Cooking time: 30 minutes | Servings: 6

Nutritional Value: Calories 274 | Total Fat 12g | Protein 34g | Carbs 6g

Ingredients:

- 1/4 teaspoon of freshly ground black pepper
- 1 tablespoon of minced garlic
- 2 tablespoons of olive oil extra-virgin
- 1 1/2 lbs. of breast fillet of chicken diced
- 1 medium-sized red bell pepper diced
- 2 tablespoons of mixed herbs fresh
- 1/4 teaspoon of Kosher salt
- 2 tomatoes diced
- 1/2 cup of tomato puree
- 1 medium onion chopped
- 4 oz. of green beans make small pieces

Instructions:

- Warm the oil inside a medium-sized nonstick skillet over a medium-high flame. Cook until the garlic and onion are fragrant.
- Cook the chicken in the pan for 7 to 8 minutes or until it is browned. Combine the bell pepper, green beans, tomatoes, tomato puree, and herbs. Cook for another 7 minutes, covered, stirring occasionally—season to taste with salt and pepper.
- Cook for about 10 minutes with the lid on, then transfer to a platter and serve immediately.

15. Turkey Breast Stuffed with Romano Basil

Preparation time: 10 minutes | **Cooking time:** 30 minutes | **Servings:** 8

Nutritional Value: Calories 402 | Total Fat 20g | Protein 53g | Carbs 1g

Ingredients:

- 1 cup of grated Romano cheese
- 4 garlic cloves minced
- 1/4 teaspoon of pepper
- 1 turkey breast bone-in (around 4 to 5 pounds)
- 2 tablespoons of olive oil extra-virgin
- 1/2 teaspoon of salt
- 4 lemon slices
- 1/2 cup of fresh basil leaves chopped

Instructions:

- Preheat your oven at 400°F
- Combine the Romano cheese, lemon slices, basil, and garlic inside a large-sized mixing bowl. Using your fingertips, gently loosen the skin from the turkey breast and stuff it with the mixture. To protect the skin on the underside of the breast, toothpicks can be used. After applying the oil, season the skin with salt and pepper.
- Bake for about 25 minutes, then serve and enjoy.

Chapter 9: Snacks and Sweets

1. Cucumber Sandwich Bites

Preparation time: 10 minutes | **Cooking time:** 0 minutes | **Servings:** 12

Nutritional Value: Calories: 187 | Fat: 12g | Carbohydrates: 4g | Protein: 8g

Ingredients:

- ¼ cup of avocado peeled, pitted & mashed
- 1 cucumber, sliced
- 8 slices of whole-wheat bread
- 1 tablespoon of chopped chives
- 2 tablespoons of soft cream cheese
- Salt & black pepper to the taste
- 1 teaspoon of mustard

Instructions:

- Spread the mashed avocado and the rest of the ingredients, except for the cucumber slices, on each piece of bread.
- Put a slice of cucumber on each piece of bread, then cut each piece of bread into thirds and put them on a tray as a snack.

2. Chocolate Rice Pudding

Preparation time: 10 minutes | **Cooking time:** 20 minutes | **Servings:** 6

Nutritional Value: Calories: 271 | Fat: 8g | Carbohydrates: 4g | Protein: 3g

Ingredients:

- 2 cups of almond milk
- 1 cup of long-grain brown rice
- ½ cup of chopped dark chocolate
- 2 tablespoons of Dutch-processed cocoa powder
- 1 teaspoon of vanilla extract
- ¼ cup of honey

Instructions:

- In the Instant Pot, mix together the almond milk, cocoa, honey, rice, and vanilla. Press the Manual button to set the timer for 20 minutes after you've closed the lid. Once the timer goes off, wait 15 minutes for the pressure to drop on its own, then quickly let out the rest of the pressure. After you close the lid, press the "Cancel" button. Serve hot with chocolate chips on top.

3. Energy Bites

Preparation time: 20 minutes | Cooking time: 0 minutes | Servings: 20

Nutritional Value: Calories: 100 | Fat: 7g | Carbohydrates: 7g | Protein: 2g

Ingredients:

- 1/3 cup of unsweetened shredded coconut
- 2 cups of cashew nuts
- ¼ teaspoon of cinnamon
- 1 teaspoon of lemon zest
- 4 tablespoons of dates, chopped
- ¾ cup of dried apricots

Instructions:

- On a baking sheet, put the parchment paper. In a food processor, pulse all of the ingredients until they are crumbly and well mixed. Make small balls out of the dough and put them on a baking sheet that has been set up. Put in the fridge for about an hour.
- Serve.

4. Asparagus Tots

Preparation time: 10 minutes | Cooking time: 25 minutes | Servings: 2 (10 tots)

Nutritional Value: Calories 78 | Total Fat 3.2g | Protein 7.5g | Carbs 6.9g

Ingredients:

- 12 ounces of asparagus trimmed and diced
- 1/2 cup of panko bread crumbs

- Cooking spray
- 1/4 cup of Parmesan cheese grated

Instructions:

- Bring salty water to a boil over a medium-high flame. Bring a pot of asparagus to a boil for about 5 minutes. Drain for 5 minutes in a colander or until it is cool enough to handle.
- Mix the asparagus, Parmesan cheese, and breadcrumbs together in a large-sized bowl. Use your hands to mix everything together until it looks like dough. Roll one tablespoon of the mixture into a ball to make a tot. Put on a serving platter. Keep doing the same thing with the rest of the mixture. Put the tater tots in the freezer for half an hour.
- Turn the oven on to 400°F.
- Spray or grease the baking sheet and the outside of the tots with cooking oil. Bake for a total of about 10 to 15 minutes.

5. Crab Cake Lettuce Cups

Preparation time: 15 minutes | Cooking time: 20 minutes | Servings: 4

Nutritional Value: Calories: 344 | Fat: 24g | Carbohydrates: 2g | Protein: 24g

Ingredients:

- 2 tablespoons of Dijon mustard
- 1 teaspoon of garlic powder
- ½ teaspoon of ground black pepper
- 1 large egg
- ¼ cup of extra-virgin olive oil
- 1 teaspoon of dried dill (optional)

- 6 tablespoons of Roasted Garlic Aioli
- ¼ cup of minced red onion
- 4 Bibb lettuce leaves, thick spine removed
- ½ cup of almond flour
- 1-pound of jumbo lump crab
- 2 teaspoons of smoked paprika
- 1 teaspoon of celery salt

Instructions:

- Before breaking up the crabmeat with a fork inside a large-sized mixing dish, remove any shells that you can see. Add the egg, 2 tablespoons of aioli, and the Dijon mustard. Mix with a fork and add the crab meat. Mix together the almond flour, red onion, dill (if you're using it), paprika, celery salt, garlic powder, and pepper. Give it 10 to 15 minutes to cool down to room temperature.

- Make eight small cakes, each about 2 inches across. Over a medium-high flame, warm the olive oil. Fry the cakes for 2 to 3 minutes on each side or until golden. Turn the flame down to low and cook for another 6 to 8 minutes or until the middle is set. Take the pan off the flame.

- Wrap two small crab cakes in a lettuce leaf and put 1 tablespoon of aioli on top of each one.

6. Almond Cardamom Cream

Preparation time: 20 minutes | **Cooking time:** 0 minutes | **Servings:** 4

Nutritional Value: Calories: 283 | Fat: 12g | Carbohydrates: 5g | Protein: 7g

Ingredients:

- 2 teaspoons of cardamom, ground
- 1 teaspoon of vanilla extract
- ½ cup of stevia
- 3 cups of almond milk
- 1 ½ cups of water
- Juice of 1 lime
- ½ cup of honey
- 1 teaspoon of rose water

Instructions:

- Blend the almond milk, cardamom, and the rest of the ingredients inside a blender until the mixture is smooth. Pour the mixture into cups and put them in the fridge for 30 minutes before serving.

7. Spanish Nougat

Preparation time: 10 minutes | **Cooking time:** 20 minutes | **Servings:** 20

Nutritional Value: Calories: 110 | Fat: 5g | Carbohydrates: 7g | Protein: 2g

Ingredients:

- 1 1/2 cups of honey
- 1 ¾ cups of almonds, roasted & chopped
- 3 egg whites

Instructions:

- In a saucepan, bring the honey to boil over a medium-high flame, then set it aside to cool. Honey and egg whites mixed together make a thick, shiny meringue. Return the mixture to a medium-high flame and cook, often stirring, for about 15 minutes.

When the color and texture change to a dark caramel, take it off the flame and stir in the almonds.

- Pour the hot mixture into an aluminum-lined 9x13-inch pan. Cover with a second piece of foil and make it as smooth as possible. Let it cool all the way down before serving. Put a wooden board on top of it and use heavy cans to hold it down. In this state, let it harden and dry for 3–4 days. Using a sharp knife, cut the dough into 1-inch squares.

8. Coriander Falafel

Preparation time: 10 minutes | **Cooking time:** 10 minutes | **Serving Size:** 8

Nutritional Fact: Calories: 122 | Fat: 6g | Carbohydrates: 12g | Protein: 3g

Ingredients:

- 1 cup of canned garbanzo beans
- ¼ teaspoon of cayenne pepper

- 1 chopped yellow onion
- 1 teaspoon of lemon juice
- Olive oil for frying
- 3 tablespoons of tapioca flour
- 1 bunch of parsley leaves
- ¼ teaspoon of baking soda
- 5 garlic cloves, minced
- 1 teaspoon of coriander, ground
- ¼ teaspoon of cumin powder
- A pinch of salt & black pepper

Instructions:

- Mix the onion, parsley, beans, and the rest of the ingredients (except the oil and flour) inside a food processor until smooth. Put the mixture into a mixing bowl and stir the flour in well. Make 16 balls out of the mixture and flatten them a little.

- Put the falafels in a pan with a medium-high flame and cook for 5 minutes on each side. Falafels can be served as a snack after any extra fat is taken off.

9. Tomatoes Stuffed with Olives and Cheese

Preparation time: 10 minutes | **Cooking time:** 0 minutes **Servings:** 24

Nutritional Value: Calories: 136 | Fat: 8g | Carbohydrates: 5g | Protein: 5g

Ingredients:

- ½ cup of crumbled feta cheese
- ¼ teaspoon of red pepper flakes
- 2 tablespoons of olive oil

- ¼ cup of mint, torn
- 2 tablespoons of black olive paste
- 24 cherry tomatoes, top cut off & insides scooped out

Instructions:

- Mix the olive paste with the rest of the ingredients, except for the cherry tomatoes, in a bowl with a whisk. Stuff this mixture into the cherry tomatoes, arrange them on a platter and serve as an appetizer.

10. Stuffed Avocado

Preparation time: 10 minutes | Cooking time: 0 minutes | Servings: 2

Nutritional Value: Calories: 233 | Fat: 9g | Carbohydrates: 11g | Protein: 6g

Ingredients:

- 1 tablespoon of chopped basil
- 2 teaspoons of pine nuts, toasted & chopped
- Salt & black pepper to the taste
- 1 avocado, halved & pitted
- 10 ounces of canned tuna, drained
- 2 tablespoons of chopped sun-dried tomatoes
- 1 ½ tablespoons of basil pesto
- 2 tablespoons of black olives, pitted & chopped

Instructions:

- Inside a mixing bowl, mix the tuna, sun-dried tomatoes, and the rest of the ingredients. (except for the avocado). The tuna mixture should go about halfway into each half of an avocado.

11. Lemon Squares

Preparation time: 30 minutes | Cooking time: 0 minutes | Servings: 4

Nutritional Value: Calories: 136 | Fat: 11g | Carbohydrates: 7g | Protein: 2g

Ingredients:

- 2 bananas, peeled & chopped
- 1 tablespoon of honey
- ¼ cup of lemon juice
- 1 cup of avocado oil+ a drizzle
- A pinch of lemon zest, grated

Instructions:

- Put the bananas and the rest of the ingredients inside a food processor and pulse till the bananas are soft. Spread the mixture on the bottom of a pan that has been oiled with a drizzle of oil. Put it in the fridge for 30 minutes to an hour before cutting it into squares and serving it.

12. Blackberry and Apple Cobbler

Preparation time: 10 minutes | Cooking time: 30 minutes | Servings: 6

Nutritional Value: Calories: 221 | Fat: 6g | Carbohydrates: 6g | Protein: 9g

Ingredients:

- ¼ cup of apples, cored & cubed

- 6 cups of blackberries
- ¼ teaspoon of baking powder
- 1 tablespoon of lime juice
- ½ cup of water
- ¾ cup of stevia
- Cooking spray
- ½ cup of almond flour
- 3 ½ tablespoons of avocado oil

Instructions:

- Mix the berries with half of the stevia and lemon juice in a bowl. Sprinkle with flour, whisk, and pour into a baking dish that has been buttered.

- In a separate bowl, mix together the flour, baking powder, the rest of the sugar, the water, and the oil with your hands. Spread the mixture on top of the berries and bake for about 30 minutes at 375°F.

- Serve hot, and enjoy.

13. Zucchini Boats

Preparation time: 10 minutes | **Cooking time:** 20 minutes | **Servings:** 12 boats

Nutritional Value: Calories 48 | Total fat 2.8g | Protein 3g | Carbs 4.1g

Ingredients:

- 1/4 medium chopped onion
- 2 tablespoons of pine nuts
- 1 teaspoon of dried oregano
- 2 chopped cloves of garlic
- 1 teaspoon of dried basil
- 1/8 cup of feta cheese crumbled

- 6 medium-sized zucchini
- 1/8 cup of diced green olives
- 1/2 cup of grated Asiago cheese, divided

Instructions:

- Set the oven rack 6 inches away from the heat source and turn on the broiler.

- Take off the ends of the zucchini and cut each squash in half lengthwise. Scrape the seeds out of the squash and put them in a bowl. In a mixing bowl, mix together the onion, basil, feta cheese, olives, garlic, pine nuts, 1/2 cup Asiago, and oregano. Stuff the mix into the zucchini shells. Put the zucchini boats on a baking sheet and sprinkle some Asiago cheese on top.

- Under a preheated broiler, cook for about 10 minutes or until the cheese has turned brown.

14. Mushrooms Filled with Spinach and Cheese

Preparation time: 10 minutes | **Cooking time:** 25 minutes | **Servings:** 8

Nutritional Value: Calories 223 | Total fat 18.8g | Protein 6.1g | Carbs 9.4g

Ingredients:

- 4 tablespoons of olive oil
- 1 package of mushrooms, stems removed (8 ounces)
- 4 tablespoons of Italian-style salad dressing
- 1 package of softened cream cheese (8 ounces)

- 4 tablespoons of Parmesan cheese grated
- 1 package of frozen spinach chopped (10 ounces)
- 1 onion chopped
- 4 tablespoons of dry bread crumbs
- 3 minced garlic cloves

Instructions:

- On all sides of each mushroom cap, spread Italian dressing.

- At 390°F, cook the mushrooms for about 5 minutes or until they are soft. Take the mushrooms out of the oven, but don't turn it off.

- Over medium-high flame, heat the oil in a pan and sauté the garlic and onion for 6 to 8 minutes or until the onion becomes soft. Mix in the Parmesan cheese, spinach, cream cheese, and 3 tablespoons of bread crumbs.

- Before you put the remaining bread crumbs on top, divide the spinach mixture evenly among the mushroom caps. Put the mushrooms back in the oven for another 10 minutes or until the tops are golden brown.

15. Veggie Fritters

Preparation time: 10 minutes | Cooking time: 10 minutes Servings: 8

Nutritional Value: Calories: 209 | Fat: 11g | Carbohydrates: 4g | Protein: 5g

Ingredients:

- ¼ teaspoon of ground coriander
- 2 teaspoons of ground cumin

- 4 chopped scallions
- 2 tablespoons of parsley, chopped
- ½ cup of almond flour
- 2 eggs, whisked
- ¼ teaspoon of lemon juice
- 2 beets, peeled & grated
- 3 tablespoons of olive oil
- Salt & black pepper to the taste
- 2 grated carrots
- ½ teaspoon of turmeric powder
- 2 minced garlic cloves
- ¼ cup of tapioca flour
- 2 chopped yellow onions

Instructions:

- Mix the garlic, scallions, onions, and the rest of the ingredients (except the oil) together in a bowl, stir well, and then form the mixture into medium-sized fritters.

- When the pan is hot, add the fritters and cook them for 5 minutes on each side over a medium-high flame.

16. Coconut Blueberry Balls

Preparation time: 15 minutes | Cooking time: 10 minutes | Servings: 12

Nutritional Value: Calories: 129 | Fat: 7g | Carbohydrates: 14g | Protein: 7g

Ingredients:

- ½ teaspoon of vanilla
- ¼ cup of flaked coconut
- ½ cup of creamy almond butter

- ¼ cup of blueberries
- 1 cup of rolled oats, gluten-free
- ¼ cup of flaxseed meal
- 1 ½ tablespoons of chia seeds
- ¼ cup of honey
- ¼ teaspoon of cinnamon

Instructions:

- Mix the oats, cinnamon, chia seeds, and flaxseed meal together well in a large-sized mixing bowl. Put almond butter in a bowl that can go in the microwave and heat it for 30 seconds. Mix the ingredients together until they are all smooth. Vanilla and honey are mixed into the melted almond butter with a whisk.

- Mix the mixtures of almond butter and oats together. Mix the blueberries and coconut in well. Make small balls out of the oat mixture and put them on a baking sheet. Put in the fridge for about an hour. Serve and enjoy.

17. Cocoa Brownies

Preparation time: 10 minutes | **Cooking time:** 20 minutes | **Servings:** 8

Nutritional Value: Calories: 200 | Fat: 4g | Carbohydrates: 9g | Protein: 4g

Ingredients:

- 4 tablespoons of almond butter
- 30 ounces of canned lentils, rinsed & drained
- ½ teaspoon of baking soda
- 1 tablespoon of honey
- 2 tablespoons of cocoa powder

- 1 banana, peeled & chopped
- Cooking spray

Instructions:

- Blend the lentils, honey, and the rest of the ingredients (except the cooking spray) in a food processor until smooth.

- Spread this out evenly in a greased baking dish and bake at 375°F for 20 minutes. Cut the brownies into pieces and serve them cold.

18. Watermelon Pizza

Preparation time: 10 minutes | **Cooking time:** 0 minutes | **Servings:** 2

Nutritional Value: Calories: 143 | Fat: 6g | Carbohydrates: 1g | Protein: 5g

Ingredients:

- 1 tablespoon of chopped fresh cilantro
- 4 tablespoons of feta cheese, crumbled
- 1 tablespoon of pomegranate sauce
- 9 oz. of the watermelon slice

Instructions:

- Crumble the Feta cheese over the watermelon slice on the platter. Add the fresh cilantro and mix. Then, a lot of pomegranate juice should be poured over the pizza. Cut the pizza into individual portions.

19. Zucchini Bites

Preparation time: 10 minutes | **Cooking time:** 25 minutes | **Servings:** 24 to 36 bites

Nutritional Value: Calories 51.3 | Total fat 3.2 g | Protein 2.3 g | Carbs 3.6 g

Ingredients:

- 3 slices of chicken finely sliced
- 1/4 cup of cream
- 1 chopped onion
- 1 cup of grated cheese
- 1 large grated zucchini
- 3 whole eggs
- 1 tablespoon of olive oil extra-virgin
- 1 large grated carrot
- 1/2 cup of self-rising flour

Instructions:

- Heat the oil in a large-sized skillet and cook the onion until it becomes clear. After the chicken has changed color, let it cook for 2 to 3 minutes before adding the zucchini and carrots. Give it a few minutes to cool down.

- In a separate medium-sized bowl, whisk together the milk, eggs, and cheese. Add the egg mixture to the zucchini mixture and stir in the flour.

- Half of the zucchini bites mixture should be put in each muffin cup.

- Bake at 350°F for about 15 to 20 minutes or until done.

20. Stewed Cinnamon Apples with Dates

Preparation time: 15 minutes | **Cooking time:** 10 minutes | **Servings:** 6

Nutritional Value: Calories: 111 | Fat: 2g | Carbohydrates: 6g | Protein: 2g

Ingredients:

- 1 teaspoon of unsalted butter
- ¼ cup of chopped pitted dates
- ½ cup of water
- 4 large apples
- ¼ teaspoon of vanilla extract
- 1 teaspoon of ground cinnamon

Instructions:

- In the Instant Pot, mix together the apples, water, dates, and cinnamon. Close the lid, let the steam out, then press the Manual button and set the timer for 3 minutes.

- When the alarm goes off, quickly release the pressure until the float valve sets. After you close the lid, press the "Cancel" button. Mix the butter and vanilla extract together. Serve either hot or cold.

Chapter 10: Sauces
Condiment and Dressing

1. Sriracha Mayo

Preparation time: 5 minutes | **Cooking time:** 0 minutes | **Servings:** 1 cup

Nutritional Value: Calories: 101 | Fat: 11g | Carbohydrates: 1g | Protein: 0.2g | Sodium: 237mg

Ingredients:

- 1 teaspoon of ground black pepper
- ¼ cup of sriracha sauce
- 1 cup of mayonnaise
- ½ tablespoon of lemon juice

Directions:

- Inside a mixing bowl, mix mayonnaise, lemon juice, sriracha sauce, & black pepper. You can serve it right away or put it in the fridge.

2. Sesame Sauce

Preparation time: 5 minutes | **Cooking time:** 10 minutes | **Servings:** 7 cups

Nutritional Value: Calories: 71 | Fat: 0.6g | Protein: 1g | Carbohydrates: 16g

Ingredients:

- 1 tablespoon of olive oil
- 3 cups of honey
- 4 1/2 teaspoons of red pepper flakes
- 1 tablespoon of sesame oil
- 2 tablespoons of minced garlic
- 1 tablespoon of sesame seeds
- 2 tablespoons of fresh ginger root minced
- 1 cup of orange juice
- 3 cups of soy sauce
- 1/2 lime juice

Instructions:

- On a medium-high flame, warm the olive oil in a large-sized skillet. Add the red pepper flakes and garlic and cook and stir them for 2 to 3 minutes until they smell good. Stir in the honey, ginger, sesame oil, orange juice, lime juice, and soy sauce. Cook for another 2–3 minutes or until everything is done.

3. Chermoula Sauce

Preparation time: 5 minutes | **Cooking time:** 10 minutes | **Servings:** 1/4 cup

Nutritional Value: Calories: 210 | Fat: 22g | Protein: 1g | Carbohydrates: 4g

Ingredients:

- 3 teaspoons of ground cumin
- 1 cup of chopped fresh cilantro
- 4 cloves of garlic chopped
- 2 teaspoons of paprika
- 1/2 cup of olive oil extra virgin
- 1/4 teaspoon of salt
- Pinch of cayenne pepper and more to taste
- 1/2 teaspoon of ground coriander
- 1 cup of fresh parsley chopped
- 1/4 cup of lemon juice freshly squeezed

Directions:

- Mix the coriander, cumin, and paprika together in a frying pan and heat for 30 to 60 seconds or until the mixture smells good.
- Add these spices and the rest of the ingredients to a food processor and pulse until the mixture is smooth.

4. French Dressing for Greek Salad

Preparation time: 5 minutes | **Cooking time:** 10 minutes | **Servings:** 6 (3/4 cup)

Nutritional Value: Calories: 113 | Fat: 12g | Protein: 0.2g | Carbohydrates: 2g

Ingredients:

- 1 clove of garlic

- 1/4 cup of wine vinegar
- 1/4 teaspoon of kosher salt
- 1 tablespoon of Greek seasoning
- 1/4 teaspoon of ground black pepper
- 1 teaspoon of lemon zest grated
- 1/4 teaspoon of Dijon mustard
- 1 tablespoon of water
- 1/4 teaspoon of white sugar
- 2 tablespoons of lemon juice
- 1/3 cup of olive oil

Instructions:

- Mix Greek seasoning and water inside a small-sized bowl and set it aside for 5 minutes or until the seasoning is soaked.
- Crush a clove of garlic with the side of a knife, then sprinkle it with kosher salt and use the side of the knife to mix the crushed garlic and salt into a paste.
- Mix the garlic mixture, wine vinegar, olive oil, lemon juice, pepper, lemon zest, Dijon mustard, and sugar together in a large bowl.

5. Ranch Yogurt Dressing

Preparation time: 5 minutes | **Cooking time:** 0 minutes | **Servings:** 2 cups

Nutritional Value: Calories: 44 | Fat: 4.6g | Protein: 0.5g | Carbohydrates: 1g

Ingredients:

- 1/4 teaspoon of sea salt
- 4 teaspoons of white wine vinegar

- 1/2 teaspoon of parsley dried
- 3/4 teaspoon of dill weed dried
- 1/4 teaspoon of ground black pepper
- 1 cup of plain Greek yogurt fat-free
- 2/3 cup of low-fat mayonnaise
- 1/2 cup of water
- 1 teaspoon of Dijon mustard
- 1/2 teaspoon of garlic powder roasted
- 1/4 teaspoon of white sugar

Instructions:

- Mix Greek yogurt, white wine vinegar, sea salt, mayonnaise, water, roasted garlic powder, Dijon mustard, dill, parsley, pepper, and sugar until smooth inside a large-sized mixing bowl.

6. Harissa Sauce

Preparation time: 10 minutes | **Cooking time:** 10 minutes | **Serving Size:** 1 cup

Nutritional Value: Calories: 26 | Fat: 2g | Protein: 1g | Carbs: 1g

Ingredients:

- 1 tablespoon of smoked paprika
- 5 cloves of peeled garlic
- 1 x red bird's eye fresh chili
- Salt and pepper to taste
- 1 x 400g can of chopped tomatoes drained (include juice for a saucy consistency)
- 2 x fresh red chilies fresh

- 5 to 6 tablespoons of olive oil
- 2 x bell peppers red/sweet pimento peppers charred and skins removed

For the spice mix:

- 2 teaspoons of coriander seeds
- 1 teaspoon of fennel seeds
- 2 teaspoons of dried chili flakes
- 1 teaspoon of cumin seeds

Directions:

- All of the spices in the spice mix should be toasted in a pan over medium flame until they smell good. After you've used a pestle and mortar to crush them until they're just right, set them aside.
- Blend or process the rest of the ingredients, including the spices, in a blender or food processor until you have a bright, brick-red paste. Add salt and pepper to taste, then put the food in jars.

7. Creamy Italian Dressing

Preparation time: 10 minutes | **Cooking time:** 0 minutes | **Serving Size:** 3 cups

Nutritional Value: Calories: 139 | Fat: 14g | Protein: 1g | Carbs: 2g

Ingredients:

- 1/4 teaspoon of garlic powder
- 2 tablespoons of red wine vinegar
- 1/8 teaspoon of ground black pepper
- 1/4 teaspoon of salt
- 1 cup of mayonnaise low-fat

- 3/4 teaspoon of Italian seasoning
- 1/2 onion small
- 1 tablespoon of white sugar

Instructions:

- Blend or process the mayonnaise, vinegar, onion, and sugar together. Add salt, garlic powder, pepper, and Italian seasoning to taste. Mix until everything is smooth.

8. Mediterranean Sauce (Lebanese Toum)

Preparation time: 10 minutes | **Cooking time:** 0 minutes | **Servings:** 2 cups

Nutritional Value: Calories: 259 | Fat: 27g | Protein: 2g | Carbs: 4g

Ingredients:

- 2 teaspoons of salt
- 48 cloves of garlic
- 330g of neutral oil (e.g., canola)
- 2 tablespoons of lemon juice
- 3 tablespoons of cold water

Directions:

- Put the garlic cloves and salt in a food processor and run it until it's smooth, stopping to scrape down the sides as needed. Pour the lemon juice in and stir until everything is well mixed.

- Slowly pour in 1/2 cup of oil while the motor is running. Put one tablespoon of water into the container. After turning off the machine, scrape both sides of it. Repeat until all the oil and water are used. By mixing, a light, fluffy

topping will be made that can be spread out at the end.

9. Balsamic Green Salad Dressing

Preparation time: 10 minutes | **Cooking time:** 0 minutes | **Servings:** 1 cup

Nutritional Value: Calories: 143 | Fat: 13.5g | Protein: 0.2g | Carbs: 6g

Ingredients:

- 2 tablespoons of brown sugar
- 1/2 cup of olive oil
- 1 tablespoon of lemon juice
- 1/2 cup of balsamic vinegar
- 5 dashes of lemon pepper

Instructions:

- Inside a bowl, mix together the oil, vinegar, sugar, lemon pepper, and lemon juice. Use a funnel to put the mixture into a clean container with a lid that fits tightly. Shake the bottle well before pouring it over your favorite green salad.

10. Blue Cheese Salad Dressing

Preparation time: 10 minutes | **Cooking time:** 0 minutes | **Servings:** 3 cups

Nutritional Value: Calories: 196 | Fat: 21g | Protein: 1.2g | Carbs: 1g

Ingredients:

- 1/2 teaspoon of salt
- 4 ounces of crumbled blue cheese

- 2 cups of salad oil
- 1 tablespoon of Worcestershire sauce
- 3 tablespoons of tarragon vinegar
- 1 small clove of garlic, chopped and peeled
- 3 tablespoons of lemon juice
- 2 tablespoons of red wine vinegar
- 1 tablespoon of yellow mustard prepared
- 1/2 teaspoon ground black pepper
- 2 tablespoons of steak sauce

Instructions:

- Mix together blue cheese, red wine vinegar, mustard, lemon juice, tarragon vinegar, Worcestershire sauce, steak sauce, salt, garlic, and pepper with an electric mixer in a large mixing bowl. Pour the salad oil in slowly until everything is well mixed. Serve at once.

11. Tzatziki Sauce

Preparation time: 10 minutes | Cooking time: 0 minutes | Servings: 3 cups

Nutritional Value: Calories: 34 | Fat: 1.2g | Protein: 1g | Carbs: 1g

Ingredients:

- 1/4 teaspoon of ground white pepper
- 4 to 5 cloves of garlic peeled and finely grated
- 1 tablespoon of Greek olive oil extra virgin
- 2 cups of Greek yogurt
- 1 teaspoon of kosher salt divided
- 3/4 partially peeled English cucumber sliced
- 1 teaspoon of white vinegar

Instructions:

- First, you should get the cucumber ready. You can use a food processor to grate the cucumbers. Toss the chicken with 1/2 teaspoon of kosher salt. Use a fine-mesh strainer over a deep dish to drain. Use cheesecloth to squeeze the grated cucumber until it is dry. Set it aside.

- Inside a large-sized bowl, mix together the garlic, white vinegar, 1/2 teaspoon of the remaining salt, and extra virgin olive oil. Stir everything together to mix.

- Mix the grated cucumber and garlic mixture together well inside a large-sized bowl. Mix in the yogurt and white pepper. Mix everything together well. After tightly covering it, put it in the fridge for a couple of hours.

- When you're ready to serve, mix the tzatziki sauce again and pour it into a bowl, then drizzle it with extra virgin olive oil.

12. Margarita Dressing

Preparation time: 10 minutes | **Cooking time:** 0 minutes | **Servings:** 7

Nutritional Value: Calories: 150 | Fat: 14g | Protein: 1g | Carbs: 6g

Ingredients:

- 1/4 cup of fresh lime juice
- 2 1/2 tablespoons of honey
- 1 1/2 teaspoons of ground cumin
- 2 teaspoons of cilantro dried
- 1/2 cup of olive oil extra-virgin
- 1/8 teaspoon of salt

Instructions:

- Whisk the olive oil, honey, lime juice, cilantro, cumin, and salt together in a small-sized cup.

13. Basil Tofu Dressing

Preparation time: 10 minutes | **Cooking time:** 0 minutes | **Servings:** 4 (1/2 cup)

Nutritional Value: Calories: 38 | Fat: 2g | Protein: 3g | Carbs: 2g

Ingredients:

- 2 tablespoons of fresh basil chopped
- 1 clove of minced garlic
- 2 tablespoons of cider vinegar
- 1 pinch of salt

- 1/2 (12 ounces) package of firm silken tofu
- 2 tablespoons of apple juice
- 1/2 teaspoon of Dijon mustard

Instructions:

- Blend the tofu, basil, cider vinegar, garlic, apple juice, Dijon mustard, and salt together in a blender till the mixture is completely smooth.

14. Hummus

Preparation time: 10 minutes | **Cooking time:** 0 minutes | **Servings:** 6

Nutritional Value: Calories: 204 | Fat: 10g | Protein: 23g | Carbs: 8g

Ingredients:

- Olive oil for drizzling
- 1/2 teaspoon of salt
- 80g of tahini
- 800g of rinsed and drained chickpeas
- Pepper
- 2 cloves of garlic
- 1 lemon juice

Instructions:

- Put all ingredients inside a food processor and pulse until smooth. If the batter is too hard to mix, add a tablespoon of water at a time until the right consistency is reached.

- Move to a mixing bowl and drizzle with olive oil. Add more salt and pepper to taste.

15. Pesto

Preparation time: 10 minutes | **Cooking time:** 15 minutes | **Servings:** 4

Nutritional Value: Calories: 93| Fat: 9g | Protein: 2g | Carbs: 1g

Ingredients:

- 1/2 lemon juice
- 1/2 cup of parmesan cheese shredded
- 2 cups of fresh basil leave packed
- 1 to 2 chopped cloves of garlic
- Black pepper and kosher salt to taste
- 1/3 cup of toasted pine nuts or walnuts
- 1/2 cup of olive oil extra virgin

Instructions:

- Quickly boil the basil. Make a bowl of ice water and put it near your

- .

stove. Put half of the water inside a small-sized saucepan and bring it to a boil. Put the basil leaves in boiling water for 5 to 10 seconds or until they wilt. To avoid cooking, use tongs to move the basil leaves into the ready-ice water.

- The basil needs to be dried well. Collect and wrap the basil leaves in a paper towel, squeezing out as much water as possible.

- To make the sauce with pesto. Mix the basil, pine nuts, garlic, and lemon juice in the bowl of a food processor with a blade. Pour the olive oil into the food processor as it is running. Don't process your basil pesto for too long if you want it to have some texture.

- Mix well after adding the Parmesan cheese. About half of a small-sized bowl should be full of the basil mixture. Sprinkle with parmesan cheese and salt and pepper to taste. Stir everything together to mix. Add a little extra virgin olive oil to the mixture if you think it's needed

12-Weeks Meal Plan

Week 1

Days	Breakfast	Lunch	Snack	Dinner
1	Summer Fruit Compote with Honeyed Greek Yogurt	Herbed Quinoa and Cauliflower Casserole	Chocolate Rice Pudding	Southwestern Catfish with Salsa
2	Hash Potatoes with Poached Eggs	Sicilian Fish Stew	Watermelon Pizza	Greens Tacos with Chickpeas & Turnips
3	Egg in an Avocado Boat	Zucchini with Rice and Tzatziki	Energy Bites	Tuna with Olive and Kale
4	Cauli Avocado Toast	Sautéed Chicken with Olives, Capers, and Lemons	Cocoa Brownies	Vegetable Couscous Curry
5	Green Shakshuka	Mediterranean Stew	Cucumber Sandwich Bites	Chicken Tomato, Bean, and Pepper Roast
6	Turkish Scrambled Eggs with Tomatoes	Tilapia with Avocado and Red Onion	Zucchini Bites	Pumpkin, Cauliflower, and Chickpeas Curry
7	Apple Muffins	Asparagus Risotto	Asparagus Tots	Salmon with Asparagus

Week 2

Days	Breakfast	Lunch	Snack	Dinner
1	Granola with Olive Oil	Tuna with Olive and Kale	Asparagus Tots	Sicilian Fish Stew

2	Cauliflower Hash Browns	Roasted Italian Vegetables	Coconut Blueberry Balls	Sautéed Chicken with Olives, Capers, and Lemons
3	Hash Potatoes with Poached Eggs	Chicken Tomato, Bean, and Pepper Roast	Zucchini Boats	Herbed Quinoa and Cauliflower Casserole
4	Breakfast Shake	Vegetable Couscous Curry	Veggie Fritters	Salmon with Fennel Salad
5	Cauli Avocado Toast	Chicken with Tomato-Balsamic Pan Sauce	Stewed Cinnamon Apples with Dates	Zucchini with Rice and Tzatziki
6	Caprese Stuffed Avocado	Arugula Salad with Figs and Walnuts	Cocoa Brownies	Tilapia with Avocado and Red Onion
7	Fluffy Courgette Omelet	Greens Tacos with Chickpeas & Turnips	Chocolate Rice Pudding	Southwestern Catfish with Salsa

Week 3

Days	Breakfast	Lunch	Snack	Dinner
1	Turkish Scrambled Eggs with Tomatoes	Chicken and Orzo Soup	Watermelon Pizza	Arugula Salad with Figs and Walnuts
2	Cauli Avocado Toast	Pumpkin, Cauliflower, and Chickpeas Curry	Energy Bites	Sautéed Chicken with Olives, Capers, and Lemons
3	Apple Muffins	Salmon with Fennel Salad	Lemon Squares	Roasted Italian Vegetables

4	Cauliflower Hash Browns	Sicilian Fish Stew	Zucchini Bites	Greens Tacos with Chickpeas & Turnips
5	Granola with Olive Oil	Vegetable Couscous Curry	Coriander Falafel	Chicken Tomato, Bean, and Pepper Roast
6	Egg in an Avocado Boat	Zucchini with Rice and Tzatziki	Cucumber Sandwich Bites	Tuna with Olive and Kale
7	Hash Potatoes with Poached Eggs	Southwestern Catfish with Salsa	Stewed Cinnamon Apples with Dates	Mediterranean Stew

Week 4

Days	Breakfast	Lunch	Snack	Dinner
1	Apple Muffins	Chicken with Tomato-Balsamic Pan Sauce	Cocoa Brownies	Cod Mushroom Stew
2	Caprese Stuffed Avocado	Sheet Pan Chicken and Veggies	Zucchini Boats	Vegetable Couscous Curry
3	Breakfast Shake	Asparagus Risotto	Asparagus Tots	Chicken Stuffed with Asparagus
4	Granola with Olive Oil	Salmon with Fennel Salad	Watermelon Pizza	Zucchini with Rice and Tzatziki
5	Fluffy Courgette Omelet	Herbed Quinoa and Cauliflower Casserole	Spanish Nougat	Sicilian Fish Stew
6	Summer Fruit Compote with	Sautéed Chicken with Olives,	Chocolate Rice Pudding	Moroccan Couscous with Chickpeas

	Honeyed Greek Yogurt	Capers, and Lemons		
7	Cauli Avocado Toast	Mediterranean Stew	Coconut Blueberry Balls	Tilapia with Avocado and Red Onion

Week 5

Days	Breakfast	Lunch	Snack	Dinner
1	Taleggio Mushroom Omelet	Chicken Tomato, Bean, and Pepper Roast	Zucchini Bites	Zucchini and Chickpeas Salad
2	Cauli Avocado Toast	Tilapia with Avocado and Red Onion	Lemon Squares	Asparagus Risotto
3	Breakfast Shake	Roasted Italian Vegetables	Watermelon Pizza	Salmon with Fennel Salad
4	Caprese Stuffed Avocado	Tuna with Olive and Kale	Cucumber Sandwich Bites	Pumpkin, Cauliflower, and Chickpeas Curry
5	Apple Muffins	Rosemary Turkey Patties	Cocoa Brownies	Chicken with Tomato-Balsamic Pan Sauce
6	Fluffy Courgette Omelet	Greens Tacos with Chickpeas & Turnips	Energy Bites	Chicken and Orzo Soup
7	Summer Fruit Compote with Honeyed Greek Yogurt	Chicken with Onions, Figs, Potatoes, and Carrots	Veggie Fritters	Moroccan Couscous with Chickpeas

Week 6

Days	Breakfast	Lunch	Snack	Dinner
1	Granola with Olive Oil	Arugula Salad with Figs and Walnuts	Coriander Falafel	Chicken with Onions, Figs, Potatoes, and Carrots
2	Cauliflower Hash Browns	Sheet Pan Chicken and Veggies	Coconut Blueberry Balls	Mediterranean Stew
3	Egg in an Avocado Boat	Chicken and Orzo Soup	Spanish Nougat	Vegetable Couscous Curry
4	Caprese Stuffed Avocado	Pumpkin, Cauliflower, and Chickpeas Curry	Cucumber Sandwich Bites	Chicken with Tomato-Balsamic Pan Sauce
5	Turkish Scrambled Eggs with Tomatoes	Salmon with Fennel Salad	Chocolate Rice Pudding	Moroccan Couscous with Chickpeas
6	Hash Potatoes with Poached Eggs	Southwestern Catfish with Salsa	Watermelon Pizza	Herbed Quinoa and Cauliflower Casserole
7	Taleggio Mushroom Omelet	Roasted Italian Vegetables	Zucchini Boats	Chicken Tomato, Bean, and Pepper Roast

Week 7

Days	Breakfast	Lunch	Snack	Dinner
1	Summer Fruit Compote with	Salmon with Asparagus	Asparagus Tots	Cod Mushroom Stew

Days	Breakfast	Lunch	Snack	Dinner
	Honeyed Greek Yogurt			
2	Fluffy Courgette Omelet	Zucchini and Chickpeas Salad	Cocoa Brownies	Sicilian Fish Stew
3	Chicken and Veggie Omelet	Tuna with Olive and Kale	Zucchini Bites	Rosemary Turkey Patties
4	Cauli Avocado Toast	Chicken Stuffed with Asparagus	Stewed Cinnamon Apples with Dates	Greens Tacos with Chickpeas & Turnips
5	Vegetable Frittata	Arugula Salad with Figs and Walnuts	Lemon Squares	Chicken and Orzo Soup
6	Caprese Stuffed Avocado	Turkey Breast Stuffed with Romano Basil	Veggie Fritters	Asparagus Risotto
7	Apple Muffins	Zucchini with Rice and Tzatziki	Energy Bites	Tilapia with Avocado and Red Onion

Week 8

Days	Breakfast	Lunch	Snack	Dinner
1	Cauliflower Hash Browns	Sheet Pan Chicken and Veggies	Watermelon Pizza	Arugula Salad with Figs and Walnuts
2	Taleggio Mushroom Omelet	Chicken with Onions, Figs, Potatoes, and Carrots	Spanish Nougat	Rosemary Turkey Patties
3	Egg in an Avocado Boat	Southwestern Catfish with Salsa	Cucumber Sandwich Bites	Roasted Italian Vegetables

4	Fluffy Courgette Omelet	Salmon with Fennel Salad	Coriander Falafel	Pumpkin, Cauliflower, and Chickpeas Curry
5	Summer Fruit Compote with Honeyed Greek Yogurt	Chicken Tomato, Bean, and Pepper Roast	Zucchini Bites	Moroccan Couscous with Chickpeas
6	Apple Muffins	Herbed Quinoa and Cauliflower Casserole	Chocolate Rice Pudding	Salmon with Asparagus
7	Breakfast Shake	Vegetable Couscous Curry	Stewed Cinnamon Apples with Dates	Sautéed Chicken with Olives, Capers, and Lemons

Week 9

Days	Breakfast	Lunch	Snack	Dinner
1	Fluffy Courgette Omelet	Spinach Rice	Mushrooms Filled with Spinach and Cheese	Chicken with Tomato-Balsamic Pan Sauce
2	Cauli Avocado Toast	Greens Tacos with Chickpeas & Turnips	Energy Bites	Turkey Breast Stuffed with Romano Basil
3	Taleggio Mushroom Omelet	Chicken Stuffed with Asparagus	Spanish Nougat	Salmon with Asparagus
4	Turkish Scrambled Eggs with Tomatoes	Sautéed Chicken with Olives, Capers, and Lemons	Veggie Fritters	Sicilian Fish Stew

5	Apple Muffins	Vegetable Couscous Curry	Watermelon Pizza	Chicken Tomato, Bean, and Pepper Roast
6	Granola with Olive Oil	Cod Mushroom Stew	Asparagus Tots	Herbed Quinoa and Cauliflower Casserole
7	Hash Potatoes with Poached Eggs	Asparagus Risotto	Coconut Blueberry Balls	Chicken with Basil-Lemon Gravy

Week 10

Days	Breakfast	Lunch	Snack	Dinner
1	Taleggio Mushroom Omelet	Sheet Pan Chicken and Veggies	Stewed Cinnamon Apples with Dates	Chicken with Onions, Figs, Potatoes, and Carrots
2	Green Shakshuka	Roasted Italian Vegetables	Crab Cake Lettuce Cups	Southwestern Catfish with Salsa
3	Fluffy Courgette Omelet	Salmon with Asparagus	Chocolate Rice Pudding	Rosemary Turkey Patties
4	Breakfast Shake	Chicken Stuffed with Asparagus	Lemon Squares	Vegetable Couscous Curry
5	Caprese Stuffed Avocado	Pumpkin, Cauliflower, and Chickpeas Curry	Mushrooms Filled with Spinach and Cheese	Tilapia with Avocado and Red Onion
6	Cauli Avocado Toast	Chicken and Orzo Soup	Energy Bites	Mediterranean Stew

7	Summer Fruit Compote with Honeyed Greek Yogurt	Chicken Tomato, Bean, and Pepper Roast	Spanish Nougat	Salmon with Fennel Salad

Week 11

Days	Breakfast	Lunch	Snack	Dinner
1	Chicken and Veggie Omelet	Salmon with Asparagus	Coriander Falafel	Rosemary Turkey Patties
2	Apple Muffins	Sheet Pan Chicken and Veggies	Zucchini Bites	Vegetable Couscous Curry
3	Cauliflower Hash Browns	Herbed Quinoa and Cauliflower Casserole	Veggie Fritters	Chicken with Onions, Figs, Potatoes, and Carrots
4	Taleggio Mushroom Omelet	Chicken with Tomato-Balsamic Pan Sauce	Cocoa Brownies	Arugula Salad with Figs and Walnuts
5	Cauli Avocado Toast	Sicilian Fish Stew	Zucchini Boats	Zucchini with Rice and Tzatziki
6	Caprese Stuffed Avocado	Cod Mushroom Stew	Asparagus Tots	Chicken Tomato, Bean, and Pepper Roast
7	Egg in an Avocado Boat	Southwestern Catfish with Salsa	Watermelon Pizza	Spinach Rice

Week 12

Days	Breakfast	Lunch	Snack	Dinner
1	Granola with Olive Oil	Chicken with Onions, Figs, Potatoes, and Carrots	Stewed Cinnamon Apples with Dates	Turkey Breast Stuffed with Romano Basil
2	Cauliflower Hash Browns	Pumpkin, Cauliflower, and Chickpeas Curry	Energy Bites	Chicken with Tomato-Balsamic Pan Sauce
3	Summer Fruit Compote with Honeyed Greek Yogurt	Rosemary Turkey Patties	Mushrooms Filled with Spinach and Cheese	Moroccan Couscous with Chickpeas
4	Hash Potatoes with Poached Eggs	Chicken Tomato, Bean, and Pepper Roast	Spanish Nougat	Herbed Quinoa and Cauliflower Casserole
5	Taleggio Mushroom Omelet	Spinach Rice	Almond Cardamom Cream	Cod Mushroom Stew
6	Cauli Avocado Toast	Asparagus Risotto	Crab Cake Lettuce Cups	Sheet Pan Chicken and Veggies
7	Fluffy Courgette Omelet	Chicken Stuffed with Asparagus	Asparagus Tots	Greens Tacos with Chickpeas & Turnips

Conversion Tables of the Various Units of Measurement

CONVERSION CHART

Liquid Measure

8 ounces =	1 cup
2 cups =	1 pint
16 ounces =	1 pint
4 cups =	1 quart
1 gill =	1/2 cup or 1/4 pint
2 pints =	1 quart
4 quarts =	1 gallon
31.5 gal. =	1 barrel
3 tsp =	1 tbsp
2 tbsp =	1/8 cup or 1 fluid ounce
4 tbsp =	1/4 cup
8 tbsp =	1/2 cup
1 pinch =	1/8 tsp or less
1 tsp =	60 drops

Conversion of US Liquid Measure to Metric System

1 fluid oz. =	29.573 milliliters
1 cup =	230 milliliters
1 quart =	.94635 liters
1 gallon =	3.7854 liters
.033814 fluid ounce =	1 milliliter
3.3814 fluid ounces =	1 deciliter
33.814 fluid oz. or 1.0567 qt.=	1 liter

Dry Measure

2 pints =	1 quart
4 quarts =	1 gallon
8 quarts =	2 gallons or 1 peck
4 pecks =	8 gallons or 1 bushel
16 ounces =	1 pound
2000 lbs. =	1 ton

Conversion of US Weight and Mass Measure to Metric System

.0353 ounces =	1 gram
1/4 ounce =	7 grams
1 ounce =	28.35 grams
4 ounces =	113.4 grams
8 ounces =	226.8 grams
1 pound =	454 grams
2.2046 pounds =	1 kilogram
.98421 long ton or 1.1023 short tons =	1 metric ton

Linear Measure

12 inches =	1 foot
3 feet =	1 yard
5.5 yards =	1 rod
40 rods =	1 furlong
8 furlongs (5280 feet) =	1 mile
6080 feet =	1 nautical mile

Conversion of US Linear Measure to Metric System

1 inch =	2.54 centimeters
1 foot =	.3048 meters
1 yard =	.9144 meters
1 mile =	1609.3 meters or 1.6093 kilometers
.03937 in. =	1 millimeter
.3937 in.=	1 centimeter
3.937 in.=	1 decimeter
39.37 in.=	1 meter
3280.8 ft. or .62137 miles =	1 kilometer

To convert a Fahrenheit temperature to Centigrade, do the following:
a. Subtract 32   b. Multiply by 5   c. Divide by 9

To convert Centigrade to Fahrenheit, do the following:
a. Multiply by 9   b. Divide by 5   c. Add 32

Conclusion

When the body is stressed or upset, its first instinct is to protect itself. Inflammation is the body's first response, whether to a foreign agent or pathogen that triggers an immune response or to a mental condition like stress that makes the body think its tissues are pathogens that must be destroyed. However, when the body's inflammatory response gets out of hand and lasts for a long time, it can lead to diseases and disorders that slowly but steadily hurt the body from the inside out.

One of the best ways to deal with this is to ensure we get enough nutrients so that our bodies have everything they need to heal themselves without any extra help. This lets our bodies work at their best and keeps us from getting sick.

The anti-inflammatory diet is easy to follow: just eat well-balanced meals to keep your body healthy. You don't need to follow a complicated or hard-to-understand diet plan to lose weight. Instead, by tracking what you eat, you can ensure you don't have any stress that could cause an inflammatory attack.

By eating a varied diet and sticking to a plan, you can make sure your body gets everything it needs without becoming dependent on any one food or group of foods. This change also helps the body build up its immune system and resistance to disease.

The Detailed information gathered in this book is all you need to get started with an anti-inflammatory diet.

The recipes listed here have been carefully put together because they use the best ingredients for the body. In addition, each of these recipes has been carefully put together in a weekly plan that gives you a chance and makes your taste buds want more.

These recipes are based on food from around the world and offer the best of what each culture offers regarding taste and health. We hope they inspire you and encourage you to live a healthy life!

Made in United States
Orlando, FL
16 September 2023

36991206R00057